HOTEL ENGINEERING

TARUN BANSAL
Faculty Coordinator,
Institute of Hotel Management, Catering and Nutrition, Lucknow

AMAN PUBLICATIONS
NEW DELHI

Published by
Rajiv Jain for Aman Publications
LG-4A, Ganpati Bhawan,
4675-B/21, Ansari Road,
Darya Ganj, Delhi - 110002
PH: 23255012, 23282127
E-mail: sshjbs@yahoo.com

First Published - 2011

Reprint - 2018

ISBN–81–8204–0671
ISBN–978-81–8204–067-0

SOLE DISTRIBUTOR
JINDAL BOOK SERVICES
LG-4A, Ganpati Bhawan,
4675-B/21, Ansari Road,
Darya Ganj, Delhi - 110002

Jacket Designed by :
S.M. Graphics

Printed by:
Sachin Printers, Delhi, India

Dedicated to

My Teacher and Mentor of Hotel Engineering

Engineer O.N. Khatri

And

Students of Hospitality and Hotel Education

PREFACE

Its great pleasure to me in presenting the book on "Hotel Engineering" a subject which is always a core of my heart. After getting experience of teaching food and beverage service and management at Institute of Hotel Management, Lucknow more than twenty years, I always personally admire the subject Hotel engineering and still have a believe that no body can operate a physical plant successfully without having fundamental knowledge of Basic Principles of Hotel Engineering. To be a successful manager one must be aware about the key issues related with a physical plant. In this book I try to attempt all the issues in detail and according to modern practices of Hotel Engineering in the hotel industry.

Book covers the complete syllabus of subject Hotel engineering dealt in various courses offered by National council for Hotel Management, State Technical Universities/ Boards and other hotel management courses offered by various affiliated agencies. The book is an output of my own teaching experience as well as discussion with the various eminent personalities of Engineering. Each lesson of the book starts with an brief introduction from the point of view of students of Hospitality and hotel education to take up the lesson as a beautiful learning experience as personally I realize that most of the students assume that again they have to study Science and Math subject which they left few years back due to some reasons. Book is an attempt to convert most of the principles of science in such a manner so a common human being also easily grasps the subject. Here I want to mention one of the best example of principles of refrigeration cycle quoted by my Hotel Engineering teacher and mentor Engineer O.N.Khatri , during the class he called one student on platform and ask him to perform jogging for a couple of minutes and really it was surprising to us why Sir ask him to do the same but we didn't made any efforts to ask question to Sir. After jogging for few minutes, student was sweating and feeling cold. Then Sir start explaining the principles of refrigeration cycle : how jogging imparts the heat in the body and leads to condensation and end result cooling that was the way he try to attempt almost all the principles of building system of a physical plant by using human engineering.

The book is divided into ten lessons and discuss all the basic principles, guidelines, concepts with numerical problems based as per the need of the lesson in a very simple way and try to make an attempt to be a life learning experience to the students of Hospitality and Hotel Education.

The book contains the following special features:

- ❖ Prepared strictly according to the syllabus of NCHMCT and various State Technical Universities/ Boards.
- ❖ Book gives due weightage to each topic according to marks and time allotted.
- ❖ It is written in very simple language.
- ❖ Book contains necessary figures, tables, charts etc to explain the subject matter in an easy to understand style.
- ❖ Book contains concept review questions so that students may test their understanding.

Book contains learning objectives in the beginning of each lesson.

ACKNOWLEDGEMENT

I am grateful to the following professionals for their invaluable help and motivation. Engineer O.N.Khatri, Mr. A.K.Singh Principal IHM Lucknow, Mr.R.K.Saxena Principal IHM Mumbai, Mrs. Suman Singh Ex- Principal IHM Lucknow, Mr. K.K. Saraf (Director F&A), Mr. M.S. Bhuie (Director Studies) National Council for Hotel Management, Mr. A.P.Rastogi (Director J.P.Institute of Hotel Mnanagement), Mr. Arun Nagarkar, Mr.N.L.Rastogi (HOD IHM Lucknow), Prof. Arun Mittal (IET Lucknow).

I also sincere thanks to my colleagues and Mrs. Manju Bose, Librarian IHM Lucknow for helping me any time and every time.

My special thanks to my family member for their love and continuous encouragement: My mother Smt. Vimla Bansal, father Late Sri Umesh Chandra Bansal, aunt Smt. Meena Agrawal, uncle Mr.Naresh Agrawal, wife Aruna Bansal, brother Adarash, brother in law Prof. Narendra Garg, Sister Mrs. Neeru Garg, sons Shubham and Harsh (Cheeku).

I am thankful to all my students for their valuable criticism and suggestions on time to time to improve inputs of the book. Constructive suggestions for improvements in the book will be gratefully acknowledged. Students should feel free to clarify their doubts by writing to me:tarun_bansal_1965@rediffmail.com.

CONTENTS

1

INTRODUCTION TO HOTEL ENGINEERING DEPARTMENT

LEARNING OBJECTIVES

By the end of the lesson you will be able to:

- Define physical plant.
- Explain maintenance work to be taken care by the hotel engineering department.
- Explain what are the new concepts and facilities available in today's hotel.
- To develop typical organization structure of hotel engineering department.
- To explain duties and responsibilitics performed hy hotel engineering personnel.
- Explain types of maintenance with its merits and demerits.

INTRODUCTION

If you are looking for a secure position in the hospitality industry, you should seriously consider becoming a chief engineer, the director of a physical plant or a head maintenance person. Management turnover for this position is minimal. Finding a competent chief engineer is very difficult task in comparison to finding a food and beverage manager/ executive housekeeper/front office manager or even a chef. The maintenance department works almost completely behind the scenes, but it fulfils a tremendously important function. The department personnel and the equipment under their control provide the atmosphere and comforts demanded by the guests.

KEY DEFINITIONS

Engineering Maintenance

It is the procedure of taking care of an equipment or machine with the view to prolong its life and also to keep it functioning at optimum efficiency throughout the useful life.

Machine

- Technically speaking machine is a mechanical arrangement, which makes work easier, that is, it provides mechanical advantage and helps to overcome large load with less effort.
- Machine can change one form of energy to another form.

Efficiency

It should be clearly understood that energy could neither be created nor destroyed. A machine will function and give the desired output energy, only if it is provided either equal or more energy but never less than the amount of output energy. The ratio of useful output power/energy to the input power/energy is defined as the efficiency of the machine. This ratio is expressed for ease as percentage and is represented by the Greek letter 'η' (eta).

- When the input to a machine is equal to the output energy/power the machine is an Ideal machine. As the input of a practical machine is always greater than the output Ideal machines are hypothetical and do not exist. Efficiency of ideal machine is unit or 100% and of the practical machine it is always less than 100%.
- In practical machines input is always greater than the output energy/power. A part of the input power/energy is utilized in the energy conversion process or the machine to work and is given out as heat, this is known as 'Un-useful output' and simply as 'Waste' or 'Loss'. The balance of the input and the loss is the 'Useful output' or simply 'Output'. The following equations describe this condition and the ratio efficiency:

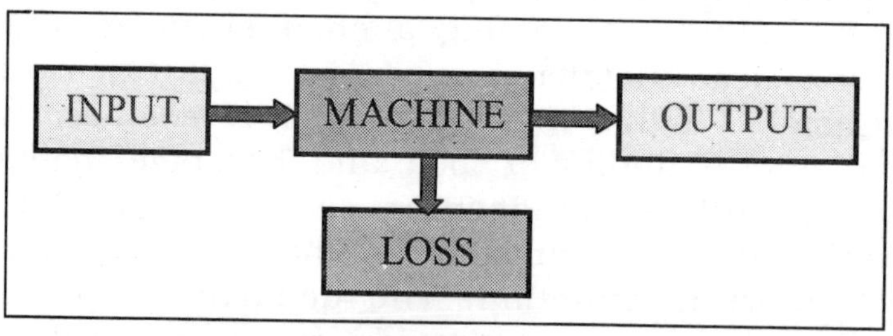

- Input to m/c = useful output + loss.
- Efficiency = Useful output/Input to machine
  = (Input − Loss)/Input
  = Useful output/Useful output + Loss.

Condition of Comfort

The condition, at which the physical and mental activity levels of a person are at the minimum possible, is the condition of comfort. Mental discomfort, irritation, and problems create mental unrest and promote physical activity and this contributes to discomfort. Similarly physical conditions when cross the permissible range produce physical discomfort and promote mental unrest and contribute to discomfort.

Maintenance Department

The science and technology of engineering and the related field of maintenance are mysteries to most people. Many managers and departments' heads realize that their businesses are dependent on the operation of their maintenance and engineering department, especially in large buildings.

Many operations define maintenance and engineering by its areas of responsibility. Other operations rely on normal dictionary definitions. Regardless of the definition or responsibilities of an organization, the basic purpose of the department can be stated as; *keeping the structure, its machines, its systems, and it products in an existing or specified state of readiness. This definition assumes that everything is kept in repair that is operating at a high efficiency level (low energy consumption), and that there are minimal breakdowns. For a hotel it means keeping guestrooms and public space salable, at a low cost.*

The maintenance and engineering department has been treated as a catchall department, which literally means that if a problem is not related to food, marketing or sales, housekeeping, or accounting, it must be a maintenance and engineering responsibility.

Physical Plant

The term physical plant refers to the grounds, building structure, building systems, interior finishes (that is paint/ wall paper and so forth) and furniture, fixtures and equipment (F.F. & E) of a lodging facility. Many of these components of the physical plant are highly visible, such as grounds, the exterior building, structure and the *furniture, fixtures and equipment.* other portion of physical plant such as structural steel in the building, the plumbing and the large routes of the heating, ventilating and air-conditioning (HVAC) system, are seldom seen by the guests or most of the employees. The elements of physical plant constitute a significant portion of the construction cost of a building and consume a significant fraction of the maintenance and energy cost incurred over the building's life time.

The care and operation of the physical plant of modern lodging facilities is largely responsibility of the engineering and maintenance department.

To understand the scope of this department's duties and responsibilities relative to physical plant, a brief overview of the physical plant of modern facilities and how these facilities have changed over time is helpful.

Essential Components of the Physical Plant

- *Estate*: land and buildings.
- Comfortable furniture/fittings to rest or work.
- *Air conditioning plant*: to maintain the temperature within the comfortable parameter.
- *Kitchen*: to take care of customers' hunger with proper taste and flavours to liking.
- *Transport system*: include lifts, escalators, a fleet of buses and taxis.
- *Audio and video system*: to entertain the customers.
- *Telecommunication system*: to receive and send massages.
- *Safety provisions*: systems, for personal safety, fire and theft.
- Staff to manage all above.

Engineering Yesterday and Today

The physical plants of simple road side motels/ hotels in the 1930's and 1940's required little more skill to maintain and operate than that needed by an owner. In contrast, the mega hotels of the late 1990's have required engineers and individuals with specialized skills for their operations.

There is a list of the systems found in the most modern lodging establishments:

- HVAC
- 24 hours hot and cold water supply
- Sewer (storm and sanitary)
- Lighting (optical fibre in many modern hotels)
- Telecommunication
- Life safety and security measures
- Vertical and horizontal transportation system
- Energy and energy management systems

Maintenance Department

as stated above hotels have to maintain a group of officers and workers whose job is to look after the various physical plants so that they are properly maintained to function without trouble and provide comfort to the customers round the clock. This group of workers constitutes the 'Engineering maintenance department'.

Objectives of the Maintenance Department

- To ascertain that the machines/equipments function at the optimum efficiency for a longer period of time.

- To target for the minimum maintenance expenditure.
- To assure that the customers can easily control the equipments to create convenient conditions to suit them.
- To assure that the customers easily operate equipments with safety.
- To assure that the machines and equipments are safe to operate by the staff.
- To ensure that the machine/equipment gives trouble free service.
- To program arrange maintenance such that there is no disturbance in the running of essential departments of the hotel.
- To program and carry out the maintenance work so that the customer is least disturbed.
- To ensure good relations and coordination with other departments and customers.

Functions of the Maintenance Department

Technical Functions

- *Upkeep of assets and establishment*: buildings, gardens, sewer and drainage, water supply, hotel roads and furniture-fittings, swimming pool.
- *Electrical maintenance*: to maintain uninterrupted electric supply and distribution. Up keep of electric wiring, lighting, and electric machines and equipments.
- *Mechanical maintenance*: maintenance of air-conditioning systems, food refrigeration and cooling machines, lifts/escalators, transport vehicles, laundry and kitchen machines and wimming pool machines.
- *Electronic maintenance*: communication system both internal and external, recreation equipments.

Executive Functions

- Planning improvements for present plant and for future plant expansion.
- Managing constructions contracts: inviting tenders, cost analysis, contract assignment, and supervision of the work in progress, testing after completion, approval, checking of bills and approving payment.
- Staff: appointment and service termination of maintenance personnel, keeping records of work efficiency and service tenure.
- Job allotment and control of the maintenance staff.
- Setting job targets and programs for the staff.
- Keeping track of the maintenance expenditure and find ways and means to reduce it.

- Maintaining coordination and friendly relation among the maintenance department and other departments of the hotel.
- Maintenance of records with respect to building and assets taxes, water tax, electricity consumption and payments, machine maintenance records, spare parts stock records, vehicles and vehicles tax records.
- To program and provide safety from fire, theft and personal safety to costumers and establishment.
- Target and program energy conservation.
- Aim for pollution control.
- Arrange for staff training and workshops and seminars to improve performance.

OPERATIONAL GOALS

When the responsibilities of the maintenance department are discussed, it is often easy to focus merely on the detail of the required activity, that is, to maintain and repair. But if we focus too narrowly on the detail, we may forget to see and appreciate the purpose of the department and its crucial role in the overall functioning of the lodging operation. A lodging property may benefit substantially if its management establishes broad goals for the hotel maintenance department. Identifying and clearly communicating such goals may help to motivate personnel, define duties and responsibilities and clarify interdepartmental relationships. The following is a sample set of general operational goals for the maintenance department which results in a functional way of viewing the department's responsibilities.

1. Protect the investment in physical plant
2. Control maintenance costs
3. Contribute as appropriate or necessary to overall guest satisfaction
4. Contribute to the efficient operation of other departments
5. Minimize the energy cost of the facility planning
6. Minimize potential safety problems

DUTIES AND RESPONSIBILITIES OF MAINTENANCE DEPARTMENT

Building and System Operation

Lodging building does not operate without continuous attention. The building and the systems installing in these buildings require basic maintenance, repair or replacement of failed parts, calibration of controls and equipment, attention to factors which may pose safety problems and inevitably a major renovation or rehabilitation. A failure to provide adequate attention to these needs can result in a poor operating performance of the building which in turn may affect guest perception of quality, employee performance and morale. The safety of the guests and employees and the profitability of the operation.

Many of the system in the building never are noticed if they are working properly. For example, an air conditioning system that is maintaining the types of indoor conditions which result in guest comfort should be almost invisible to the guest. It is the failure of systems to work properly which draws unwanted attention and create managerial nightmares.

Building Maintenance

The actual physical structure of the building may initially seem like something which requires relatively little effort on the part of the engineering department. The stone, brick, asphalt, and steel of the most of the building would appear last for ever. However, there are a large number of basic maintenance activities which must be undertaken if the building is to preserve its initial appearance and function. Approximate 5% of the Principle of Management budget is spent on non-labor aspects of building maintenance. The environment around building sometimes results in rapid deterioration of building surfaces. In some urban areas, the exterior surfaces suffer pitting and erosion due to materials in the air, cleaning of exterior surfaces may be repaired, but the engineer must be certain that the cure will not be worse than the disease since the use of some cleaning materials result damages of surfaces. Other types of maintenance include the application of protcctive materials to surfaces to retard corrosion and repel the attack of moisture entrained pollutants. The element of building maintenance which is unavoidable and continual problem is roofing. Whether it is the repair of minor leaks or the de-roofing of the entire building (a capital cost), roofing system maintenance is important concern.

Building

Building is the structure, which provides us living space, shelter and place to rest; it protects us from intruders, adverse climatic conditions and provides privacy.

Hotel is classified as a commercial building, where tourists and travelers take temporary shelter in comfortable environment of their choice.

Main Components of building: the main components of the building are listed below with their functions in short:

Foundation

Foundation is the portion of the building structure, which is built under the ground. The main functions and maintenance are as follows:

- It provides the building a firm hold with the ground and stability to the structure; it prevents the building from shifting and turning over.

- It distributes the total load of the building structure and its content evenly on the ground and thus prevents sinking.
- It provides an even level for the upper structures in spite an uneven ground.
- Maintenance: being an underground structure all possible precautions should be taken before hand during the design and construction. Modifications, repairs and maintenance in the foundation structure after the construction of the building are difficult to undertake.
  - It should be made of proper design.
  - Firm concrete base should be provided under the foundation to prevent displacement of soil due to building weight.
  - Anti termite (white-ant) treatment should be done under the foundation before construction.

Plinth

The visible structural part of the building above the foundation and below the floor level is known as Plinth. According to local conditions, the plinth is made of specified height above the ground.

- It raises the height of floor level from the ground level.
- Prevents the entry of ground water in the house.
- Checks easy access of insects and small animals.
- Maintenance:
  - Repairs of plaster as and when required.

Damp Proof Course

Damp Proof Course is a layer of impervious material, which cuts off the capillary rise of water in the building floor and walls. It prevents dampness in the building.

Floor

Building floor is smooth clean and hard levelled surface under the walls. It supports the occupants, furniture and is used as a convenient movement area in the building.

- Components of floor
  - Base: generally of waterproof cement concrete.
  - Top: of desired material: mud, brick, cement sand mortar, stone-slab etc.
- Maintenance: the floors do wear or crack due to continuous use. The following actions are taken to maintain conditions of the floors.

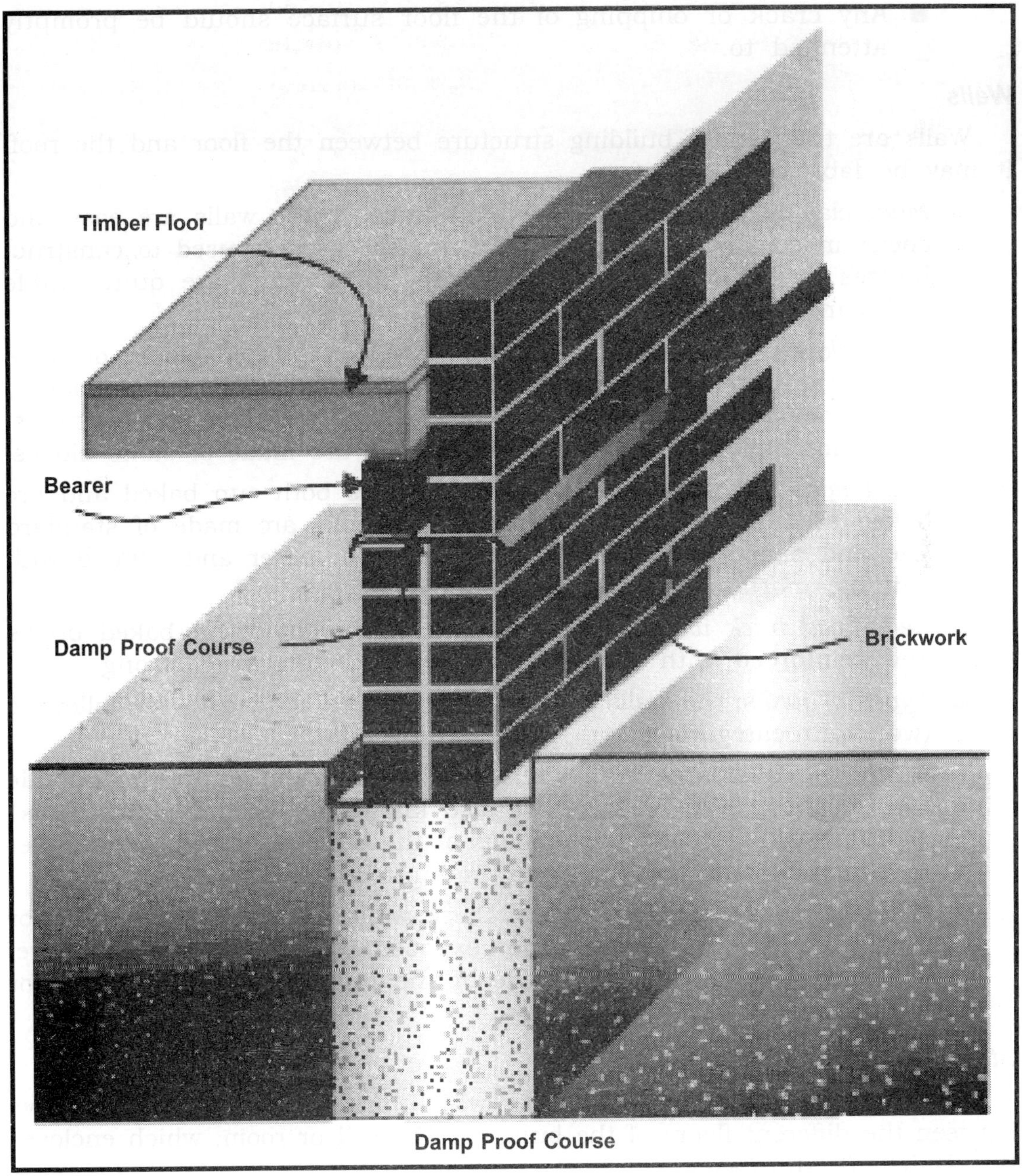

- Daily dry sweeping and wet sweeping to remove dirt and dust. This helps to prevent scratching and maintain smoothness of the surface.
- Scheduled washing with mild soap solution to remove oil and grease, which tarnish the polish, and with time harm the surface by producing acids on disintegration.

- Any crack or chipping of the floor surface should be promptly attended to.

Walls

Walls are the part of building structure between the floor and the roof. It may be fabricated out of:

- *Mud*: clay is used to fabricate mud walls. These walls are easy and cheap in construction. These walls are successfully used to construct houses in hamlets. If properly made, these walls are quite stable and can stand rains.
- *Stone-blocks*: walls are made of unfinished or finished blocks of stone layers one over other and joined with suitable bonding materials by filling the gaps. Such walls are very strong and can last centuries. Important buildings, forts and monuments are made of stone blocks.
- *Dried mud blocks (bricks)*: dried mud blocks both sun baked and fire baked are use to construct walls. The blocks are made of standard size and shape. Bricks are layered one over other and bonded with suitable mortar to make strong walls.
- *Reinforced brick walls*: these walls are made out of fire-baked bricks and reinforced with steel bars. Such walls are very strong.
- *Types of walls*: the walls of a building can be divided in the following two main categories:
  - *Outer walls*: are those walls, which are exposed to the outside atmosphere. These walls are also known as 'Load Bearing Walls'. These walls protect the inmates of the building from adverse outer climatic conditions, dangers and intruders.
  - *Inner walls or Partition walls*: these walls are made in the interior of the building and are not exposed to the outer atmosphere. These walls divide the inside of the building in proper cells for convenient use and privacy.

Stair and Staircase

Stairs are stepped inclined plane, which provide the facility to move between the different floors of the building. The cell or room, which encloses the stairs, is staircase.

Doors

Doors are opening in the walls flushed with the floor level for the entry and exit in the building or different rooms of the building. The height and width of the doors are designed for convenient use. With suitable shutters, doors are also used as barriers for entry and exit

Windows

Windows are suitable size openings in the walls at a suitable height from the floor. Their function is to maintain air ventilation to keep the interior atmosphere of the building fresh.

Ventilators

Ventilators are small openings or windows placed higher up in the wall near the roof level. They help to expel the hot stale air of the room to outside.

Window Shades

Window Shades are slab projections at the side and top of the windows to restrict entry of rain and direct sunlight in the building.

Parapet

Parapet is the low protecting wall along the edge of the roof of the building.

Subsidiary Components Of Building are listed below:

- Wall and ceiling plaster or facing and waterproofing.
- Floor plaster or facing and waterproofing.
- Drains and sewers.
- Water supply arrangement and water piping.
- Electric supply arrangement and electric wiring.
- Doors and windows frames and leaves.
- Open land and garden.
- Boundary walls and main entrance gate.

Materials Generally Used For Building Construction

- *Ballast*: Brick ballast; Stone ballast coarse and fine.
- *Sand*: Coarse; Fine.
- *Building blocks*: Stones; Bricks.
- *Facing materials*: Stone slabs or tiles; Plastic Tiles; Plastic granules; Cement sand plaster.
- *Bonding paste materials*: Portland cement; Lime; Ash; Sand; Water.
- Ø *Reinforcing materials*: Steel sections.
- Ø *Pipes and Pipefitting*: for water supply system.
- Ø *Electric wiring material, accessories and fittings*: for electric supply system.
- Ø *Timber wood*: for doors and windows frames and leaves.

Parapet

Maintenance of Guestrooms, Furnishings and Fixtures

From the perspective of the lodging property guest, the guestrooms, furnishings and fixtures of the property are very visible features which contribute to the overall experience of the establishment either positively or negatively. The proper maintenance of these elements is usually a direct responsibility of the engineering department staff. Since these elements receive a lot of use, they are often replaced within first ten years (a capital expenditure). The department replaces the items itself or supervises outside contractors, the yearly expenditures on the maintenance of guestrooms, furnishings and fixtures of the establishment are charged against the *POM ACCOUNT. About 2-3 % of the total POM is spent on furniture and 2.5- 4.5% on painting and decorating.*

Equipment Maintenance and Repair

The amount of equipment installed in a modern hotel or motel is astounding. in the guest room there are television, HVAC Unit, various electric lamps, ventilation fans, in the bath sanitary fittings and sundry other items. Public spaces have HVAC units with fans, chillers, pumps and lighting. Pools have pumps, filters, water treatment systems and more. The kitchen and laundry are full of equipment requiring almost continual repair and adjustment. The repair and maintenance of all the equipment is the responsibility of the engineering department. Maintenance means to maintain something or is to keep in an existing state or to preserve from failure or decline. Unfortunately with respect to equipment a large fraction of the time spent in some engineering operations is directed at repair rather than at maintenance. Repair expenses have a significant effect on the cost of building maintenance.

The cost of equipment repair and maintenance includes the cost of parts and supplies for building equipment and the cost of labour used in the repair of equipment. Approximately 12% of the property POM budget is directly expended for electrical and mechanical equipment maintenance.

Budgeting and Cost Control

Approximately 11% of the property POM budget is directly expended for accurate to budget and cost control. Unfortunately at many establishments the development and control of this budget is not approached with the same level of care and analysis that is used in other areas.

Security/Safety Maintenance

Security involves physical assets of the property, employees, suppliers and the guests while safety involves the potential injury to both employees and guests. At smaller establishments, it is not unusual for building safety and security to be largely the responsibility of the engineering department. Some specific safety and security concerns with exist within the engineering area including key control, lock rotation, control of tools and supplies, emergency response to fires and other potentially dangerous situations, safe operations of equipment and tools and outside contractor interactions.

Contractual and Regularity Compliance

The term Contractual and regularity compliance refer to requirements imposed upon the property which are of a legal nature and are some times directly or indirectly the responsibility of engineering. National, state and local governments are involved in establishing these requirements as are unions with in the property and contractors. Some of the requirements are imposed by the Governments which are entirely or partially the responsibility of engineering include elevator inspections, and certification of fire code compliance, building code compliance, health/ sanitary code compliance, environmental protection agency compliance and occupational safety and health compliance.

The contractual responsibilities of engineering pertain to those contracts as part of their maintenance department budget for work to be performed by outside vendors. The maintenance department may also for periodic calibration of control, fire alarms and communication systems. Outside contract for water treatment, trash removal, fire extinguishers charging, cleaning and painting of kitchen duct work and maintenance of major pieces of HVAC equipment are also common.

Besides these basic maintenance contracts, major work to renovate or repair the building and grounds will also be contracted but is likely to be considered as a capital investment and handled separately from the POM budget.

Parts Inventory and Control

The nature of the work performed in maintenance results in a need for parts and supplied which are unique in many instances. The uniqueness of these parts or supplies may mean they require long lead times when they are ordered. However, the ability to operate portions of the facility safely and comfortably often requires immediate access to parts or supplies in order to affect repairs. For this reason an adequate parts and supplies inventory and control over the purchase and storage of these items are very important.

Renovations, Additions and Restorations

The need to redecorate and renovate whether because of wear and tear caused by use, because of changing needs for space or in order to support a new concept is a common feature of all lodging properties. For many lodging chains expenditures in these areas are greater each year than the expenditure on new properties. Depending on the magnitude of the project and the organization of the property and company the work performed in some or all of these tasks may be the responsibility of the property's maintenance department. The responsibility may include the actual performance of the work or the supervision of outside contractors as they perform the necessary tasks.

Special Projects

With the introduction of new technologies and the needs of lodging customers to special services, the engineering department is called upon to perform many special projects. For example: new communication, solar system, water treatment plant, optical fiber lighting etc.

Special events may require the construction of display stands, protective barriers. Trade shows may require additional electric services, phone connection and special lightings. These projects require the input of the engineering department early in the negotiating stages of the contract for the event to ensure that costs are recovered and that the necessary services are ready to use for the customers upon their arrival.

Training of Staff

The training activities within the maintenance area may differ some what from those in other areas of the property, many people hired in the maintenance department (electricians, painters, carpenters) already possess specific skills or abilities. While some responsibility exists to maintain their skill levels, the primary focus of training is to inform these employees the standards and specific requirement of the property at which they are employed. This training may be grouped in the categories of general training, departmental training and job-specific training.

Coordination of Hotel Engineering Departments with Other Departments

Engineering department of a hotel is required to be in constant contact with other departments of the hotel for the following reasons:

- Maintenance of building, furniture, fixture and equipments.
- To ensure supply of audio–video equipment whenever needed for conferencing, banquet functions.
- Maintenance and smooth functioning of Building system such as HVAC, Lighting, music, water, transport, etc.
- Renovation, restoration program. Of various key areas of hotel.
- Staff training and induction.
- Concern with correcting the trouble or fault that might occur any time during the functioning of equipment or machine.

Hotel Engineering Department Coordinates With Following Major Department
Food and Beverage Service
Food and Beverage Production
Front Office
Accommodation Operations
Human Resource
Accounts and Finance
Safety and Security
Kitchen Stewarding
Purchase and Stores

Job Description of Chief Engineer

Job title : Chief engineer

Reporting to : General manger

Responsible for : All hotel engineering staff

Job Summary

Responsible for overall financial, technical and administration of hotel engineering department.

Job Responsibility

- To give proper directives and instructions to the subordinate staff.
- To check efficiency of building and system operation.
- To ensure maintenance of hotel building, guestrooms, furnishings and fixtures, equipment, security / Safety maintenance.
- To coordinate with financial controller for Budgeting and cost control.
- To dealt with Contractual and regularity compliance.
- To keep a track on inventory and control.
- To take decisions about renovations, additions and restorations.
- Submission of proposal, and execution of Special projects.
- To ensure proper Training and induction of maintenance staff.
- To coordinates with Heads of other department.
- To draw and check work program.

- To conduct meetings with his staff.
- To ensure guests satisfaction.

Importance of Records in Maintenance Department

Maintenance process is neither static nor lifeless. Its patterns are ever changing with time, situations, environment and how the operators handle and operate the equipments.

The patterns of the maintenance procedures depend on the followings;

- The type and quality of the machine installed.
- The quality of the spare parts fitted during regular maintenance.
- The quality of the maintenance work procedure.
- The maintenance schedules adopted.
- The environment of the machine.
- Operators' handling methods.
- Availability of spares at proper time.

To keep track of the above proper records are to be maintained in respect of the following:

- Management policy: to keep track of the management policy the following records:
- Records of the maintenance staff.
- Instructions issued to staff from time to time.
- The performance records for each individual staff.
- Records of cost control.
- Records of bills and payment in respect of Building, electric energy and water consumption and other expenditures.
- Records of system and system components:
- Construction drawings of buildings.
- Water supply and sewer pipe system drawings.
- Electric distribution lines and building wiring drawings.
- Machine drawings and specifications.
- Catalogues and part list of installed machines.
- Records of major overhauls.
- History records of every machine.
- Record of maintenance schedules and procedures:
- Records of instructions of the procedures to be followed during maintenance.

- Frequency of maintenance.
- Records of running and idle periods.
- Records of season start and shutdown (air conditioning plant).
- Inspection dates and observation records.
- Central record file (master record file):
- Inventory data.
- Records of procedures in respect of inspection operation and schedules.
- Records in respect of maintenance work and time involved.
- Records of replacements.
- Records of unproductive machine time.
- Records of cost involved in maintenance.
- Records of taxes and bills paid.

ORGANIZATION STRUCTURE

The maintenance department is organized to provide services to the guests and the remainder of the department within lodging facility. In order to provide the services, the staff of the department must accomplish functions that fall into two categories: technical and managerial functions. The technical functions for example: repairing of chiller, interior finishes, maintenance of equipment, land escaping etc while the managerial functions for example: preparing the budget, training etc.

The success of the department in accomplishing the technical functions is totally dependent on the performance of the department in the managerial functions which are similar to those functions necessary for the operation of the department. Maintenance managers (whether the director of maintenance in a very large first class property or the head maintenance person in a small budget property) must have the ability to perform the typical management functions of planning, organizing, directing, staffing, setting goals, motivating their staff, communication with their staff and the rest of the property and developing their staff. All of this is accomplished through departmental structure that is appropriate to the size of property.

The number of employees in the maintenance department is influenced by the property size and the maintenance alternatives selected by the manager. Larger properties, with will average 4.2 employees per 100 occupied guest rooms or 3.1 employees per 100 available guest rooms.

TYPES OF MAINTENANCE

Routine Maintenance

Routine maintenance activities are those which pertain to the general upkeep of the property, recur on a regularly basis and require relatively

ORGANISATION STRUCTURE OF HOTEL ENGINEERING DEPARTMENT OF A LARGE HOTEL

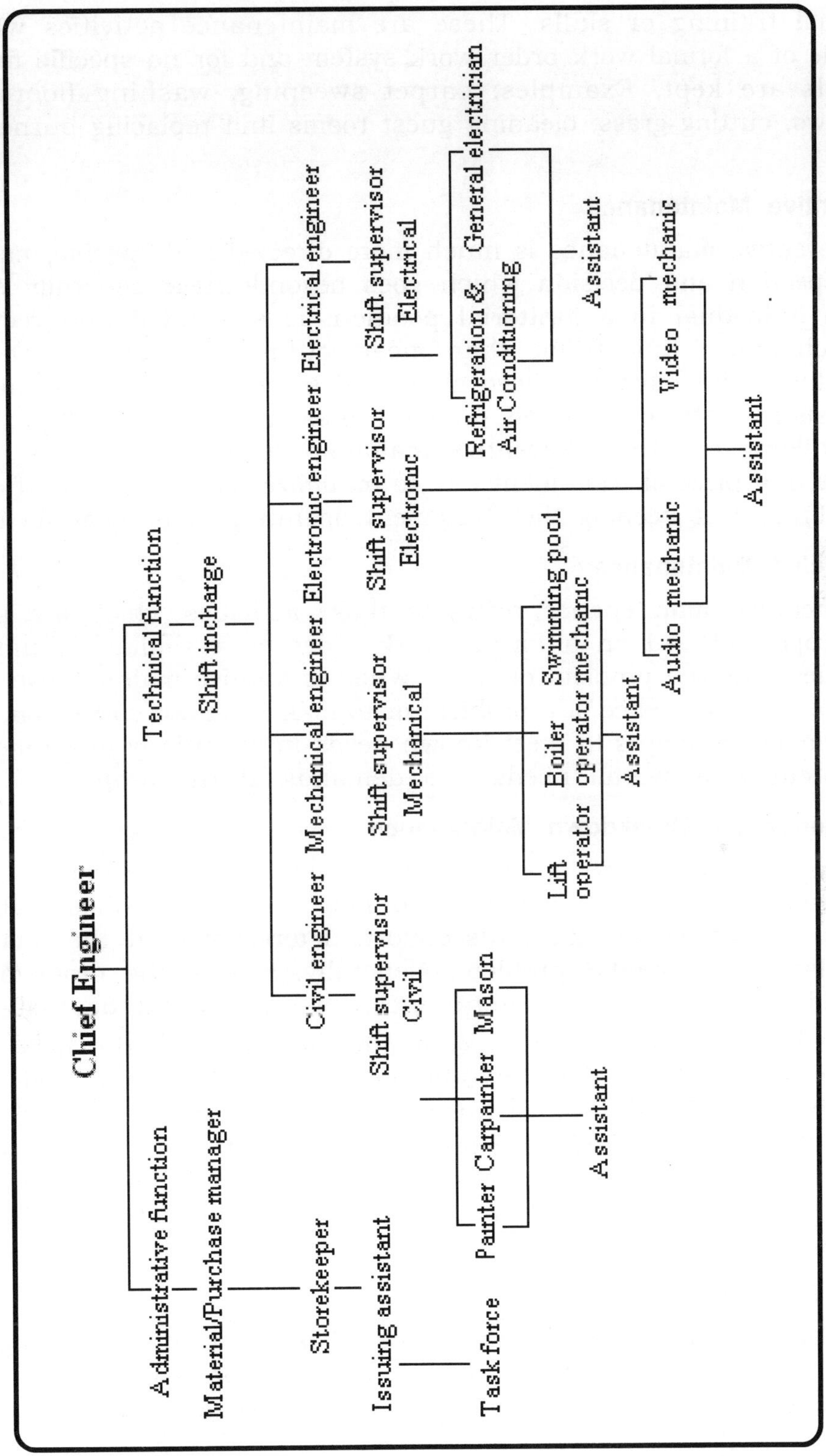

minimal training or skills. These are maintenance activities which occur outside of a formal work order work system and for no specific maintenance records are kept. Examples: carpet sweeping, washing floors, cleaning windows, cutting grass, cleaning guest rooms and replacing burned out light bulbs.

Preventive Maintenance

Preventive maintenance is much more directed and specific, has elements of inspection and decision which goes beyond those generally engaged in by an individual in a janitorial position, is scheduled and recurs within a much longer time frame than most routine maintenance and requires individuals with more advanced skills and training. Activities in maintenance are usually performed based on guidelines from equipment suppliers and the building engineer. Preventive maintenance includes actions to prolong the life of a piece of equipment and to minimize the breakdown of equipment. It is directed at keeping the equipment operating at or near its rated level.

Scheduled Maintenance

Scheduled maintenance refers to those activities which are initiated at the property based on a formal work order or a similar document which identifies a known problem or need. While preventive maintenance is initiated to delay the occurrence of a problem or to make a minor correction, scheduled maintenance attempts to meet known needs in an orderly and timely manner consistent with overall needs and demands at the property.

Emergency and Breakdown Maintenance

It is most expensive maintenance service since it generally requires a disruption of scheduled activity and may result in problem which could remove for service or cause discomfort, deterioration in the quality of the workplace, or a similar problem. Generally, solving the problem could be delayed but the level of general inconvenience would be high.

Breakdown maintenance is generally agreed to be the most expensive form of maintenance since in addition to the cost of the repair, there is often the potential for loss of business or production as a result. This type of maintenance results when a piece of equipment or a structure component completely fails. There is essentially no leeway in the scheduling of this maintenance- the equipment must be repaired immediately or the operation will be shut down.

Guest Room Maintenance

Guest room maintenance has a special meaning in the lodging industry. As it is used in many operations, it refers to preventive maintenance. In others, it takes on more characteristics of scheduled maintenance. In whatever capacity it is an important maintenance. For the guest, the guestroom is one of the most visible elements of the lodging experience. The condition and proper operation of furniture, fixtures and equipment, the appearance of ceiling and walls, the condition of carpets and floor coverings and the cleanliness of the exteriors of windows are all included in the maintenance and repair of guestrooms.

Contract Maintenance

The decision is to perform maintenance with in house personnel or to contract this maintenance is usually under the control of the engineering manager. There are potential advantages and disadvantages to contract maintenance services.

Definition of Contract

Contract is defined as an agreement, between two or more persons (known as parties) to function in unison (united) to accomplish a job. The contract invariably follows proposals from one or more parties (proposors) and its acceptance by other parties (acceptors).

Potential advantages are as follows:

1. Reduction of total labour costs.
2. Reduction of cost of supplies and equipment
3. Use of latest techniques and methods
4. Savings in administrative times
5. Flexibility to meet emergencies or changes in needs
6. Removal of the need to negotiate with labour unions
7. Removal of the need to recruit and train employees
8. Persons and experts of different fields get an opportunity to work together.
9. The job is completed in a better and efficient manner.
10. Improved quality of the job is obtained.
11. Sharing of job responsibility by the partners reduces the completion time.
12. The partners share the profit or loss according to the agreed terms.
13. Less burden on partners due to shared responsibilities.
14. The approximate cost is known before hand and it is easier to arrange fund.

Potential disadvantages are as follows:

1. False labour cost savings unless staffing levels are actually reduced.

2. Gradual escalation in total costs without property level monitoring or control.
3. Managerial laziness resulting in a failure to negotiate the best price for the service.
4. Unavailability of employees for other tasks.
5. Loss of control over employees.
6. Loss of contact with the needs of facility and staff.

- A contract, of course, is an agreement in legal form between the owner of a building and the general contractor who is responsible for the erection of the building. He, in turn, may sublet parts of his contract to subcontractors. Thus, the subcontractor will undoubtedly do the various tasks. The form which the general contract may take will follow one or a combination of several patterns:
- Unregistered Mutual contract: under this contract, the parties agree mutually without registration and with or without any intermediately. This contract system is of two types:
  - Verbal contract: is the contract in which the terms are settled verbally amongst the parties. In case of breach of the contract terms by any party, the aggrieved party will be at loss to appeal in the court of law. Verbal contract has no legal validity.
  - Written contract: under this contract system the terms are agreed in writing on paper before two witnesses. In case of breach of contract by any of the party the aggrieved parties may appeal in the court of law putting forward the written proof. The court may refuse to hear the petition, as unregistered written contract has no legal validity.
  - Merits
    - Such contracts are easily settled among parties without any cost.

2

FUELS USED IN CATERING INDUSTRY

LEARNING OBJECTIVES

By the end of the lesson you will be able to:

- Define fuel.
- Explain types of fuel with their characteristics
- Calculate requirement of fuel with its cost

INTRODUCTION

Fuel, substance that reacts chemically with another to produce heat, or that produces heat by nuclear processes. The term *fuel* is generally limited to those substances that burn readily in air or oxygen, emitting large quantities of heat. Fuels are used for heating, for the production of steam for heating and power purposes.

BASIC DEFINITIONS AND TECHNICAL TERMS

Heat

It is a form of energy and can be converted to other forms of energy i.e, steam, mechanical etc.

Temperature

It indicated hotness or coldness and also a measure of heat intensity. It is measured by using degree Celsius or degree *Fahrenheit.*

We also can convert degree Celsius into degree *Fahrenheit.* or vice versa by using a simple formula:

$9\ C = 5\ (F-32)$

For example: you want to convert 100 degree Celsius into—degree *Fahrenheit.*

Then

9 × 100 = 5 (F-32)

900 = 5 F-160

5F = 900 + 160

5F = 1060

F = 1060/5

F = 220

It means 100 degree Celsius = 220 degree *Fahrenheit.*

Striking Back

This applies to aerated type gas burners and is caused by the gas being ignited at the air vent hole of the burner, causing the flame at the burner head to be luminous with disturbed combustion.

Causes of Striking Back

Incorrect lighting by placing lighter flame too close to the burner.

Incorrect gas/air adjustment.

Dirty burners causing gas starvation at gas/air adjustment.

Rough interior of burner tube.

Transference of Heat

There are three techniques of heat transfer namely as conduction, convection and radiation.

Conduction

It means traveling of heat through a solid, or from one solid to another, provided they are in contact. You can experience it by keeping your frying pan on fire, after some time you will find that frying pan is becoming hot. All metals are good conductors of heat. Bad conductors of heat are cork, plastic, chinaware, wood; cotton and these materials are used for manufacturing of certain articles or parts of articles which require to be kept cool.

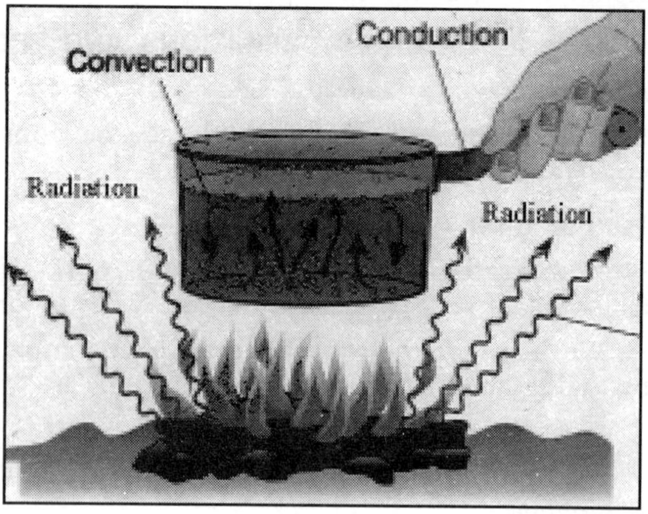

Convection

Convection is the passage of heat through liquids and gases, e.g. a kettle of water being heated; the water at the bottom becomes heated first and then because it is lighter rises to top and the heavier cold water takes its place at the bottom.

Radiation

In this, hot body loses its heat and cold body receives it through some medium, e.g. we get heat from the Sun by means of heat radiation through air as a medium.

Heat Units

British Thermal Unit

Fuel efficiency or heating value of a fuel is usually measured in terms of the number of Btu (British Thermal Unit) that are produced when a given amount of the fuel is burned under standard conditions. Heating values for solid and liquid fuels are stated in terms of Btu per lb, and values for gases in Btu per cu ft.

Scientifically, one Btu is the amount of heat needed to raise the temperature of one pound of water one degree Fahrenheit.

1 B.T.U. = 0.252 Kcal = 0.556 CHU (Centesimal Heat Unit)

1 Kcal = 2.21 CHU = 3.97 B.T.U

In practice an average of 600 Btu are required to heat 1 pint (16oz) of water from cold to boiling point.

Calorific Value of Fuels

Approximate higher heating values of common fuels are:

Solid Fuels (Btu per lb)

- Coal 12,000 to 15,000
- Lignite 6000 to 7400
- Coke 12,400
- Dry wood 8500

Liquid Fuels (Btu per lb)

- Alcohol 11,000
- Fuel oil 19,000
- Gasoline 20,750
- Kerosene 19,800

Gaseous Fuels (Btu per cu ft)

- Acetylene 1480
- Blast-furnace gas 93
- Carbon monoxide 317
- Coke-oven gas or coal gas about 600; hydrogen 319
- Natural gas 1050 to 2220
- Oil gas 516
- Producer gas 136.

TYPES OF FUELS

Solid Fuels

The common solid fuels, in order of heat potential, are coal, coke, wood, sugarcane and peat. Combustion of these causes decomposition of the fuel and evolution of the volatile matter as a gas that may burn with a sooty flame. The solid carbonaceous residue burns at a rate determined by the diffusion of oxygen to the surface. This latter combustion requires a higher surface temperature, about 400° to 800° C (about 752° to 1472° F), which is obtained by radiation of heat from the hot products or from hot surroundings. If the fuel is burned on a grate, air is forced through a bed of solid fuel particles, and the necessary temperature is maintained by inter-particle radiation.

Liquid Fuels

Common liquid fuels are oils, gasoline's, and naphtha's derived from petroleum , and to a lesser extent, coal tar, alcohol and benzol obtained from coke manufacturer.

Gaseous Fuel

Fuel, any combustible gaseous mixture used as fuel to provide energy for domestic or industrial use. Fuel gases consist principally of hydrocarbons, that is, of molecular compounds of carbon and hydrogen. The properties of the various gases depend on the number and arrangement of the carbon and hydrogen atoms within their molecules. All these gases are odorless in the pure state, and carbon monoxide is toxic. It is therefore common practice to add sulfur compounds to manufactured gas; such sulfur compounds, which are sometimes normally present in the gas, have an unpleasant smell and serve to give warning of a leak in the supply lines or gas appliance. In addition to their combustible components most gases have varying amounts of noncombustible nitrogen and water as their end products.

The devices used to burn gas for either heat or illumination consist of a burner nozzle and some means of mixing air with the gas before it reaches the nozzle, as, for example, in the Bunsen burner invented by British chemist and physicist Michael Faraday improved and popularized by German chemist Robert Wilhelm Bunsen. It works on the principle on which gas is now used in stoves and lights. By arranging more supply of air to the gas fuel perfect combustion resulted inside the burner. The non luminous flame is very hot and does not give off any smoke. Hottest part of the flame of burner is the outside edge of the outer cone.

Burners may be high and low pressure gas supply type. Maximum pressure is 14 inches water column pressure and 16000 B.T.U units per hour.. Heat output depends on pressure. Low pressure is 4 inch water column and have 18000 B.T.U. units per hour, output, so, low pressure burners output is more than high pressure burners. Gas burner: it is the part of the gas stove, which mixes proper amount of air with the gas and thus help proper combustion of the mixture at the top. The body is made of cast iron, while the burner top is made of cast iron or brass.

The parts of the burner and their function are listed below:

- ❖ Gas receiving tube: it is fixed in front of the gas nozzle opening of the manifold. Holes are provided on the tube surface for the sucking of air.
- ❖ Venturi section: when the bore of a tube is restricted in a specially designed curved manner. A specially designed restricted bore of a tube is a Venturi. When a fluid flows in the tube, Venturi creates a low-pressure zone and out side fluid is sucked in the Venturi tube. When the gas flowing in the tube reaches the Venturi section low pressure is created. This helps suction of the out side air through the holes at the Venturi section.
- ❖ Mixing section: further extension of the gas tube helps the mixing of the gas and air. This extension is known as mixing tube. The mixing tube opens in a gas uptake pipe.
- ❖ Gas uptake pipe: this is a double cylinder construction with a full-length hole in the center. The cavity between the cylinders is closed at the bottom and open at the top.
- ❖ Burner top: a burner top is placed on the top of the uptake pipe. The burner-top has holes on its surface. Gas and air mixture comes out through these holes and burns when ignited.
- ❖ The central opening supplies extra air to the inside of the flame for proper burning. It also keeps cool the uptake pipe to prevent 'BACK FIRING' due to over heating of the gas-air mixture in the uptake pipe.

Pressure Regulator

The pressure regulator reduces the high pressure of the cylinder gas to a constant low-pressure supply to the gas appliance. The following are the main parts of the regulator:

- Regulator body: the body of the regulator is divided in two sections:
  - Lower section: the lower sections is made up of the following parts:
    - An extended neck at the bottom to fix the regulator on the cylinder valve assembly.
    - Locking and gas opening knob: The knob is provided on the extended neck. A quarter clockwise-turn of the knob locks the regulator on the valve assembly. A further quarter-turn of the knob presses the cylinder pin valve and allows gas to enter the regulator through a specially designed opening known as valve seat at the base of the lower section.
    - Gas outlet nozzle: is provided at the side of the lower section. This outlet is connected to the burner manifold pipe inlet with a rubber tube or steel pipe.
  - Upper section: contains the following parts:
    - Pressure regulating spring: a spring is provided in the upper section to press the diaphragm.
    - Spring Pressure regulating nut: is provided at the top of the section. It adjusts the pressure of the spring on the diaphragm. The pressure nut is factory adjusted and sealed.
  - Rubber diaphragm: a strong rubberized canvas diaphragm is inserted and tightened between the upper and lower sections of the regulator. The spring presses the diaphragm on the top.
  - Specially designed valve: it is hooded at the lower side of the diaphragm. This valve sits on the underside of the valve seat from where the gas can enter in the lower section below the diaphragm.
- Regulator working:
  - Turning the regulator knob press-opens the cylinder pin valve, gas enters at full pressure in the lower section presses and lifts the diaphragm against the spring pressure. The lift of the diaphragm pulls up the valve on the seat to close the entry of the gas.
  - The opening of the burner knob releases the gas pressure under the diaphragm in the lower section of regulator

- The spring now presses the diaphragm down and opens the valve and allows gas to enter in the lower section from the cylinder.
- The spring and diaphragm then adjust at such a position as to allow required quantity of gas to the burner at constant recommended pressure.

Fossil Fuels, energy-rich substances that have formed from long-buried plants and microorganisms. Fossil fuels, which include petroleum, coal, and natural gas, provide most of the energy that powers modern industrial society. The gasoline that fuels our cars, the coal that powers many electrical plants, and the natural gas that heats our homes are all fossil fuels.

Chemically, fossil fuels consist largely of hydrocarbons, which are compounds composed of hydrogen and carbon. Some fossil fuels also contain smaller amounts of other compounds. Hydrocarbons form from ancient living organisms that were buried under layers of sediment millions of years ago. As accumulating sediment layers exerted increasing heat and pressure, the remains of the organisms gradually transformed into hydrocarbons. The most commonly used fossil fuels are petroleum, coal, and natural gas. These substances are extracted from the earth's crust and, if necessary, refined into suitable fuel products, such as gasoline, heating oil, and kerosene. Some of these hydrocarbons may also be processed into plastics, chemicals, lubricants, and other non-fuel products. Geologists have identified other types of hydrocarbon-rich deposits that can serve as fuels. Such deposits, which include oil shale, tar sands, and gas hydrates, are not widely used because they are too costly to extract and refine. The majority of fossil fuels are used in the transportation, manufacturing, residential heating, and electric-power generation industries.

Combustion

Combustion, process of rapid oxidation or burning of a substance with simultaneous evolution of heat and, usually, light. In the case of common fuels, the process is one of chemical combination with atmospheric oxygen to produce as the principal products carbon dioxide, carbon monoxide, and water, together with products such as sulfur dioxide that may be generated by the minor constituents of the fuel. The term *combustion,* however, also embraces oxidation in the broad chemical sense, and the oxidizing agent may be nitric acid, certain perchlorates, or even chlorine or fluorine.

Problems Associated with Fossil Fuels

Acid rain and global warming are two of the most serious environmental issues related to large-scale fossil fuel combustion. Other environmental problems, such as land reclamation and oil spills, are also associated with the mining and transporting of fossil fuels.

Comparative study of fuels based on their characteristics

Type of fuel	Controllability of heat output	Cleanliness	Smoke emission	Fuel storage
Coal	Fairly good if the draught is thermostatically controlled	Not clean	Considerable smoke emission unless very carefully fired	1 cu.ft of storage space holds 560000 B.t.u of potential heat. The bunker must be closed to boiler.
Anthracite	As above	As above	smokeless	1 cu.ft of storage space holds 700000 B.t.u of potential heat. The bunker must be closed to boiler.
Coke	As above	As above	smokeless	1 cu.ft of storage space holds 300000 B.t.u of potential heat. The bunker must be closed to boiler.
Oil	Very good	Fairly clean	Normally smokeless except when being started up or when incorrectly fired	1 cu.ft of storage space holds 10,000,00 B.t.u of potential heat. The need to provide a special tank increases capital cost of the plant. The tank can be sited wherever convenient.
Gas	Very good	Completely clean	smokeless	No storage required
Electricity	Excellent	Completely clean	Smokeless	No storage required

Note: From above study we can select gas and electricity are best fuels for hotel and catering industry but we should also remember that if any breakdown happens in case of electricity than specialist attention is required which might not be immediate available. The price varies of gas and electricity in proportion to the cost of solid fuel.

When fossil fuels are burned, sulfur, nitrogen, and carbon combine with oxygen to form compounds known as *oxides.* When these oxides are released into the air, they react chemically with atmospheric water vapor, forming sulfuric acid, nitric acid, and carbonic acid, respectively. These acid-containing water vapors—commonly known as acid rain—enter the water cycle and can subsequently harm the biological quality of forests, soils, lakes, and streams.

Ash Particles

Combustion of fossil fuels produces unburned fuel particles, known as ash. In the past, coal-fired power plants have emitted large amounts of ash into the atmosphere. However, government regulations also require that emissions containing ash be scrubbed or that particles otherwise be trapped to reduce this source of air pollution. While petroleum and natural gas generate less ash than coal, air pollution from fuel ash produced by automobiles may be a problem in cities where diesel and gasoline vehicles are concentrated.

Global Warming

Carbon dioxide is a major by-product of fossil fuel combustion, and it is what scientists call a greenhouse gas. Greenhouse gases absorb solar heat reflected off the earth's surface and retain this heat, keeping the earth warm and habitable for living organisms. Rapid industrialization through the 19th and 20th centuries, however, has resulted in increasing fossil fuel emissions, raising the percentage of carbon dioxide in the atmosphere by about 28 percent. This dramatic increase in carbon dioxide has led some scientists to predict a global warming scenario that could cause numerous environmental problems, including disrupted weather patterns and polar ice cap melting.

Comparative Fuel Cost

Fuel cost can be calculated by using the following formulae, inserting current prices of all four fuels and arriving at the cost of a useful "therm" in each case.

1 Therm = 100000 Btu

(Btu is a measure of heat)

Coke

If coke cost Rs.12000 per ton

Therefore 1 lb costs Rs.4.00

Coke produces 12 000 Btu per lb

Therefore 1 therm costs–cost per lb + 100000/12000

$$\frac{4+100000}{12000} = \text{Rs.}33.33$$

A useful therm is the amount of heat output to good use. Coke is calculated to be 60% efficient.

Therefore a useful therm costs= cost per therm + 100/60

33.33 + 100/60 = Rs. 55.55

Gas

To change cubic feet into therms you must know the heating power or calorific value (CV) of the gas. This will be shown on the gas cylinder and the simple calculation for working out the amount of heat supplied is:

Therms = Calorific value × hundreds of cubic feet/1000

A useful therm is the amount of heat output to good use. Gas is calculated to be 80% efficient.

Therefore a useful therm costs= cost per therm × 100/80 = Rs. X

Electricity

1 unit of electricity produces 3412 Btu

Electricity is calculated to be 100* efficient

Therefore 1 therm costs = cost per unit × 100 000/3412 = Rs x

Oil

1 gallon produces 165000 Btu

Oil is calculated to be 75% efficient

Therefore 1 therm costs= Cost per gallon × 100000/165000

1 useful therm = cost per therm × 100/75 = Rs. X

Summary

Oil, gas and coal are the most usual fuel for large scale use. Although electricity is used for cooking as well as heating purpose in most of the hotels and catering units of India. The basic idea is to provide information about different types of fuels used in the hotel and catering industry and consumption pattern varies from hotel to hotel as per its location and volume of production of food.

Concept Review Questions

1. Enlist types of fuels used in hotel and catering industry.
2. Being a manager of a catering unit on what basis you will take decisions about utilization of fuels.
3. Explain safety precautions while handling with solid fuels.

4. Discuss Advantages of electricity as a fuel on liquid fuel.

Numerical Problems

1. Consumption pattern of different types of fuels used in a catering unit are as follows. Determine costs of these fuels and recommend how you can control cost of the fuels as a chef of this catering unit.

LPG commercial cylinder 60/month

Electricity consumption in kitchen 2200 KwH/Month

Coal consumption 4500 Kgm/month

Project Assignments

1. Discuss with the chef of a hotel about their installed kitchen equipment and submit a report with its merits and demerits on the basis of utilization fuels and cost aspect.
2. Survey various large institutional and industrial catering units of your city and submit a report how they can reduce fuel costs by using latest techniques of food production.

3

AUDIO-VIDEO EQUIPMENTS

LEARNING OBJECTIVES

By the end of the lesson you will be able to:

- Understand basic fundamentals of audio-video equipment
- Explain types of audio video equipment used in hotel industry
- Explain functioning of television
- Explain different types of telephones in hotel and catering industry
- Explain types of computers and functioning of computers
- Explain role of internet in hotel and catering industry
- Explain equipments used in conferences/ seminars

INTRODUCTION

Audio video equipments, in its widest sense, are as old as mankind's need for ways and means of exchanging information over long distances. In ancient times and during the middle ages, visual signals were usually employed for the purpose, in the form of beacon fires lit on top of towers or on hills and visible a long way off. (As these you can see in films or on particular destination). Of course, a limited number of prearranged messages could be communicated by such means. Signaling by means of flags or lamps (may you have seen on railway platforms), and the hoisting and lowering of signal balls, as are commonly employed in navigation, also belong to general category of communication by visual signals. Now a days we have hundreds of such equipments by which we can pass any type of information any where in the world in couple of seconds. Google earth search engine provide the information of any area of the world just by using a click of mouse and latest techniques are developed recently by ISRO and they are launching "BHUVAN" by which you can get information of any place of the world and they said that they can provide not only map of any the place of the world but also all relevant facts required by you.

Technology is changing vary fast so this topic is an attempt just to develop very basic knowledge about all these equipments in very brief. Students are advised to update themselves on time to time with new upcoming equipments so can facilitate your guests in a perfect manner.

TELEVISION

Television has a variety of applications in society, business, and science. The most common use of television is as a source of information and entertainment for viewers in their homes. Security personnel also use televisions to monitor buildings, manufacturing plants, and numerous public facilities. Public utility employees use television to monitor the condition of an underground sewer line, using a camera attached to a robot arm or remote-control vehicle. Doctors can probe the interior of a human body with a microscopic television camera without having to conduct major surgery on the patient. Educators use television to reach students throughout the world. video conferencing is the most modern used of this equipment by which one person can address or communicate with his/her counterparts from one place to his/her colleagues on hundreds of different destinations.

Television, system of sending and receiving pictures and sound by means of electronic signals transmitted through wires and optical fibers or by electromagnetic radiation. These signals are usually broadcast from a central source, a television station, to reception devices such as television sets in homes or relay stations such as those used by cable television service providers. Television is the most widespread form of communication in the world. Though most people will never meet the leader of a country, travel to the moon, or participate in a war, they can observe these experiences through the images on their television.

A television program is created by focusing a television camera on a scene. The camera changes light from the scene into an electric signal, called the video signal, which varies depending on the strength, or brightness, of light received from each part of the scene. In color television, the camera produces an electric signal that varies depending on the strength of each color of light.

Satellite transmissions are used to efficiently distribute television and radio programs from one geographic location to another by networks; cable companies; individual broadcasters; program providers; and industrial, educational, and other organizations. Programs intended for specific subscribers are scrambled so that only the intended recipients, with appropriate decoders, can receive the program.

The first practical television system began operating in the 1940s.

COMPUTERS AND INTERNET

As online computer systems become more popular, televisions and computers are increasingly integrated. Such technologies combine the capabilities of personal computers, television, DVD players, and in some cases telephones, and greatly expand the kinds of services that can be provided. For example, computer-like hard drives in set-top recorders automatically store a TV program as it is being received so that the consumer can pause live TV, replay a scene, or skip ahead. For programs that consumers want to record for future viewing, a hard drive makes it possible to store a number of shows. Some set-top devices offer Internet access through a dial-up modem or broadband connection. Others allow the consumer to browse the World Wide Web on their TV screen. When a device has a hard drive and a broadband connection, consumers may be able to download a specific program, opening the way for true video on demand.

Consumers may eventually need only one system or device, known as an information appliance, which they could use for entertainment, communication, shopping, and banking in the convenience of their home. One type of network, a local area network (LAN), consists of several PCs or workstations connected to a special computer called a server, often within the same building or office complex. The server stores and manages programs and data. A server often contains all of a networked group's data and enables LAN workstations or PCs to be set up without large storage capabilities. In this scenario, each PC may have "local" memory (for example, a hard drive) specific to itself, but the bulk of storage resides on the server. This reduces the cost of the workstation or PC because less expensive computers can be purchased, and it simplifies the maintenance of software because the software resides only on the server rather than on each individual workstation or PC.

Mainframe computers and supercomputers commonly are networked. They may be connected to PCs, workstations, or terminals that have no computational abilities of their own. These "dumb" terminals are used only to enter data into, or receive output from, the central computer.

The Internet is a mammoth resource of data, programs, and utilities. American computer scientist Vinton Cerf was largely responsible for creating the Internet in 1973 as part of the United States Department of Defense Advanced Research Projects Agency (DARPA). In 1984 the development of Internet technology was turned over to private, government, and scientific agencies. The World Wide Web, developed in the 1980s by British physicist Timothy Berners-Lee, is a system of information resources accessed primarily through the Internet. Users can obtain a variety of information in the form of text, graphics, sounds, or video. These data are extensively cross-indexed, enabling users to browse (transfer their attention from one information site to another) via buttons, highlighted text, or sophisticated searching software known as search engines.

Wide area networks (WANs) are networks that span large geographical areas. Computers can connect to these networks to use facilities in another city or country. For example, a person in Mumbai can browse through the computerized archives of the National council for hotel management in New Delhi. The largest WAN is the Internet, a global consortium of networks linked by common communication programs and *protocols* (a set of established standards that enable computers to communicate with each other).

TELEPHONE

Telephone, instrument that sends and receives voice messages and data. Telephones convert speech and data to electrical energy, which is sent great distances. All telephones are linked by complex switching systems called central offices or exchanges, which establish the pathway for information to travel. Telephones are used for casual conversations, to conduct business, and to summon help in an emergency (as in the 100 service in the India). The telephone has other uses that do not involve one person talking to another, including paying bills (the caller uses the telephone to communicate with a bank's distant computer) and retrieving messages from an answering machine. About half of the information passing through telephone lines occurs entirely between special-purpose telephones, such as computers with modems. A modem converts the digital bits of a computer's output to an audio tone, which is then converted to an electrical signal and passed over telephone lines to be decoded by a modem attached to a computer at the receiving end. Another special-purpose telephone is a facsimile machine, or fax machine, which produces a duplicate of a document at a distant point.

Private Branch Exchange

A large business will usually have its own switching machine called a Private Branch Exchange (PBX), with hundreds or possibly thousands of lines, all of which can be reached by dialing one number. The extension telephones connected to the large business's PBX are often identical to the simple single-line instruments used in residences. The telephones used by small businesses, which do not have their own PBX, must incorporate the capability of accessing several telephone lines and are called multiline sets. The small-business environment usually requires the capability of transferring calls from one set to another as well as intercom calls, which allow one employee to call another without using an outside telephone line.

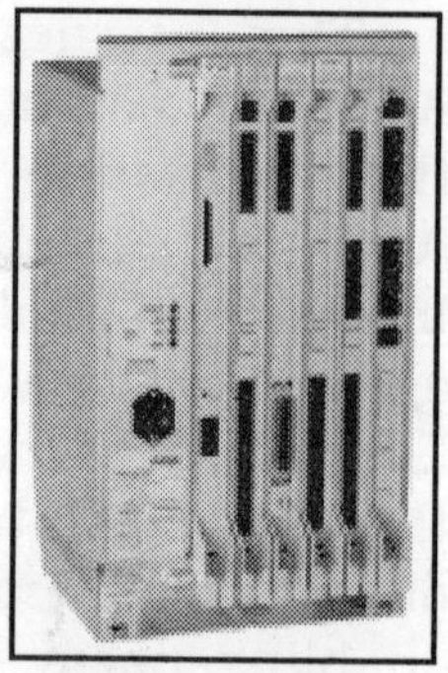

CELLULAR TELEPHONE

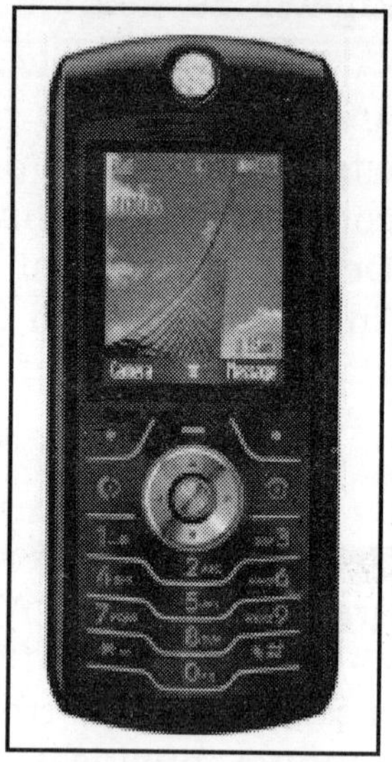

A cellular telephone is designed to give the user maximum freedom of movement while using a telephone. A cellular telephone uses radio signals to communicate between the set and an antenna. The served area is divided into cells something like a honeycomb and an antenna is placed within each cell and connected by telephone lines to one exchange devoted to cellular-telephone calls. This exchange connects cellular telephones to one another or transfers the call to a regular exchange if the call is between a cellular telephone and a no cellular telephone. The special cellular exchange, through computer control, selects the antenna closest to the telephone when service is requested. As the telephone roams, the exchange automatically determines when to change the serving cell based on the power of the radio signal received simultaneously at adjacent sites. This change occurs without interrupting conversation. Practical power considerations limit the distance between the telephone and the nearest cellular antenna, and since cellular phones use radio signals, it is very easy for unauthorized people to access communications carried out over cellular phones. Currently, digital cellular phones are gaining in popularity because the radio signals are harder to intercept and decode.

The introduction of radio into the telephone set has been the most important recent development in telephone technology, permitting first the cordless phone and now the cellular phone. In addition to regular telephone service, modern cellular phones also provide wireless Internet connections, enabling users to send and receive electronic mail and search the World Wide Web.

Answering machines and phones with dials that remember several stored numbers (repertory dials) have been available for decades, but because of their expense and unreliability were never as popular as they are today.

Multifunctional telephones that use microprocessors and integrated circuits have overcome both these barriers to make repertory dials a standard feature in most phones sold today. Many multifunctional telephones also include automatic answering and message-recording capability.

Videophones are devices that use a miniature video camera to send images as well as voice communication. Videophones can be connected to regular telephone lines or their messages can be sent via wireless technology. Since the transmission of a picture requires much more bandwidth (a measure of the amount of data a system can transmit per period of time) than the transmission of voice, the high cost of transmission facilities has limited the use of videophone service. Video service is now used to hold business "teleconferences" between groups in distant cities using high-capacity transmission paths with wide bandwidth. Videophones suitable for conversations between individuals over the normal network are commercially available, but because they provide a picture inferior to that of a television set, have not proven very popular. Television news organizations adopted the use of videophones to cover breaking news stories in remote areas.

CONFERENCE/SEMINAR EQUIPMENTS

Liquid Crystal Display

It is just flat screen monitor of computer. LCD screen are filled with particular liquid which reflects light. When the screen is scanned by a computer, necessary image can be seen on the screen.

Laptops

These are portable computers which can be operated even placing it over ones "lap". It looks like a small briefcase and very conveniently put to invaluable use.

Overhead Projector

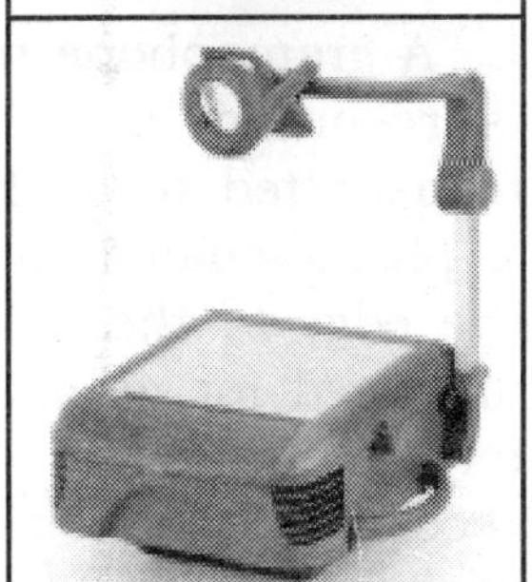

A modern concept of visual equipment which combines the benefits of a black/ white board with a projector. The lecture writes on a transparent sheet by using special transparency pen and the matter is projected on a large screen. The merits of this equipment that projection can be enlarge or reduce as per the strength of the audience.

Slide Projector

This is visual equipment in which slides are inserted into a slide tray according to a particular sequence. This round or linear tray is inserted into a projector which flashes according to the sequence. The round variety is called"carousal". The trainer controls the change of slides from one to another. Its principal parts the light source with a concave collecting mirror, the condenser and the projection lens. The source of light usually an incandescent lamp with a coiled filament emits lights in all directions.

Epidiascope

A projector which is unique. It can project any written material (paper prints, pages of books, etc.) on an opaque sheet or flat surface.

Loudspeaker

A loudspeaker is a device for converting variations of electric energy into corresponding variations of acoustic energy i.e. sound. Its task is similar to the telephone receiver except the sound is produced mush more loudly. All the loudspeakers use the electrodynamics principle for the conversion of electrical oscillation into mechanical vibrations which in turns sound waves in the air.

Tape Recorder

Many broadcasts are repeated by using this device. In this sounds are recorded on magnetic tape. To produce a tape recording, the sound is converted into corresponding electric signals by means of a microphone in conjunction with amplifier equipment. These electric signals produce variations in the strength of a magnetic field. The signals are thereby recorded on a magnetic tape which is magnetized along its length in accordance with the signals impressed on it.

Gramophone Record

A gramophone record or disc is a circular plastic disc on which the sound is recorded on a spiral groove. The sound vibrations of the air can be transmitted to a sharp recording cutter which scratches a wavy groove into a plastic-coated metal disc, the cutter being guided in a spiral path from the edge to the centre of the disc. A fairly wide range of synthetic materials are used for gramophone record; the vinyl plastics are most commonly used for the purpose, e.g. polyvinyl chloride. These are so called "unbreakable" records. The moulding of records is done under pressure, with the help of heat.

Summary

Technology is changing vary fast so this topic is an attempt just to develop very basic knowledge about all these equipments in very brief. Students are advised to update themselves on time to time with new upcoming equipments. Care and cleaning of audio video equipments may preferably be done through appropriate professionals. The maintenance programs of these equipments are highly expert area and may recommend it on contract basis. A general cleaning can perform by semi-skilled mechanics. Manufacturers instructions should be adhere during the process of cleaning of the equipment.

Concept Review Questions

1. Enlist types of audio–video equipment used in most modern hotel and catering industry.
2. Write short notes on:
   1. Computer
   2. Telephone
   3. Overhead projector
   4. Slide projector
   5. Epidiascope
   6. Loudspeaker
3. Discuss functions of:

   Television

   Opaque projector

   Business phone

   Cellular phone
4. Being a manager of banquet facilities recommend list of audio-video equipment requirement for an international work shop on Facility planning which is required to be broadcasted in South Asian countries.
5. An oil company wants to demonstrate their products to their distributors. Suggest requirement audio video equipment for same purpose.

PROJECT ASSIGNMENTS

Discuss with a chief engineer of a five star hotel about their installed audio video equipments and prepare a report and compare this report with another hotel property.

Prepare a report on types of audio video equipment available in the malls of your city.

Discuss with faculty about the use of these equipments to develop a safe and secure hotel.

How audio video equipments can be used to monitor performance of the employees.

Prepare a catalogue on audio video equipment and exhibit in your class room.

4

ELECTRICAL NETWORK ENGINEERING

LEARNING OBJECTIVES

By the end of the lesson you will be able to:

- ❖ Understand basic fundamentals of electrical engineering.
- ❖ Explain types of wire with their characteristics
- ❖ Explain different types of fixtures used in hotel and catering industry
- ❖ Explain single phase and three phase ac supply
- ❖ Explain types of lighting
- ❖ Calculate amount of bill incurred on electricity consumption
- ❖ Explain safety in handling electrical equipment

INTRODUCTION

Hospitality and service industries require and use vast amounts of electric energy. Cost of electricity is increasing rapidly and it has become almost three times with in last five years. Every manager spends a lot in energy cost in comparison to other operating costs of the establishment. Dependence on a single source of energy cannot be underestimated. The industry is dependent on electricity for power, light and heat and the most of the building systems operate electrically and the value of electric energy in industries is almost impossible to determine accurately. There are two kinds of electric current: direct and alternating. The former is not often used in hotels, except occasionally for special equipment. Most electricity for the public supply is produced in the form alternating current on the three phase system.

BASIC DEFINITIONS AND TECHNICAL TERMS

Conductor

A conductor is a substance through which electricity flows freely, e.g. copper, aluminum, water or the wiring system of a building.

Volts

It measures the *pressure of flow* of an electric current. Before electricity can flow through a wire, the electric pressure at one end of the wire must be greater than at the other end: this is known as "potential difference".

One Volt

One volt is defined as potential difference necessary between the ends of a conductor whose resistance is 1 ohm, to produce a current of 1 ampere.

220 volts is introduced as the standard for domestic use and 415 volts for industrial use throughout the country.

Ohms

It measures the resistance of a conductor to the flow of a current. All conductors offer some resistance, but the lower the resistance the better the conductor. A thin wire offers more resistance (causing voltage drop) than a thick cable of same material, and therefore long runs of the former should be avoided when planning the electrical wiring of a building.

Ohm's Law

The Ohm's Law defines the relation between the above three parameters of the electric circuit as follows:

> "The voltage drop across the load resistance of the circuit is directly proportional to the current flowing through it; provided the physical parameters viz. length, cross-section, temperature and material of the load resistance remains same."

❖ Mathematical representation:

$V \alpha I$

= [R] * I [where R is a constant of proportionality and known as 'Resistance' responsible for energy waste]

- ❑ Unit of 'V' expressed in Volts.
- ❑ Unit of 'I' expressed in Ampere.
- ❑ Unit of 'R' expressed in Ohm unit.

❖ The 'V.I.R.' triangle easily recalls the circuit parameters.

Ampere

It measures the rate of flow of a current, i.e. the amount of electricity that is passing through the circuit. If an electric wire using 10 amps is plugged into a 5-amp. Socket, the demand will overstrain the circuit and should blow the fuse.

One Ampere=1Coulomb/second=1/1.6×10^{-19} electrons/second=flow of 6.25×10^{18} electrons/ second.

Watts

It measures power that is to say, the amount of electricity used by an appliance.

1000 watts = 1 kilowatt ("kW")

A unit is familiar term, is kilowatt- hour. This is the amount of current consumed, for example, by one 1,000 – watt appliance in use for one hour, or two 500 – watt appliance in use for one hour, or two 250 –watt appliance in use for two hours.

One unit produces 3,415 British Thermal Units of heat.

One B.T.U.

It is the quantity of heat required to raise the temperature of 1 lb. of water through 1 degree Fahrenheit.

There is a simple relationship between volts, ohms, amperes and watts that can be expressed by the following equations:

1. volts/ohms = amperes

For example: when the voltages of the main supply is 240 volts and the wire and other connections leading to a socket outlet have a resistance of 48 ohms, the socket outlet is able to supply 5 amps.

2. watts = amperes × volts

For example: a 5 amp. Socket using a current of 220 volt can supply an electrical appliance rated at 1,100 watts

3. amperes = watts/volts

For example: four 100-watt lamps using 220 volts could be safely supplied by a 2-amp plug.

The abbreviations used by electrical engineers are: E=volts, I=amperes, R=ohms, W=watts.

Effects of Electric Current

The flow of charge or electric current through a conductor produced the following effects:

- *Thermal effect*: The flow of electric current produces heat and causes rise of temperature of the resistive conductor.
- *Luminous effect*: Due to the thermal effect at high temperature the resistive conductor radiates light.
- *Magnetic effect*: The current flow in a conductor always accompanies with production magnetic lines of force.
- *Chemical effect*: Electric current flowing through electrolytes (water solution of salts) or molten salts causes chemical change.

Heating Effect

- ❖ Potential difference in volts unit between two points is equivalent to work involved in Joules to move one Coulomb charge through the two points.

Work = Potential difference in Volts * One Coulomb

Work – One Joule = One Volt * One coulomb

Work – One Joule/second = One Volt * One Coulomb/second

Work Rate – One watt = One Volt * One Ampere

Energy or Work/Sec. (power) = V * I Joules/second or watt = V^2/R watt = I^2 * R watt

Ø Total energy in T sec. = Power * Time in seconds

= Watt * seconds = V * I * t Joules

= V * I * t/4.2 cal [4.2 Joules = One calor

= 0.24 * V * I * t cal = 0.24 *

Electric Wires and Types of Wiring

The standard form of a wire consists of a core containing the conductor wires preferably copper which are protected and insulated by vulcanized rubber (V.R.I.), polythene, or polyvynyl chloride (P.V.C.), the purpose of insulator is to confinc clectric flow to the conductor. Wire color coding is used so that the electrician can identify the different wires when connecting them at two or more locations within a building. The diameter of the conductor determines the number of amperes it can safely carry. Insulation types and thickness specify the maximum voltage the wire can handle. Insulation type and thickness will also vary because of the environment the wire may be exposed to. When specifying wires, you must specify the normal or expected environment. Wires are generally rated in amperes.

Cables

Several conductors, each with its separate insulation, can be combined with additional insulation to form a cable. Cables must be protected against physical damage such as pressure, cutting, rubbing, dampness or attack by rodents. One method is to cover them with a strong, protective sheath. The various types of sheathed cable include the following:

- ❖ Tough – rubber sheathed (T.R.S.), also known as cab-tyre sheathed (C.T.S.) - because of outer sheath of tough rubber or cab- tyre. These wires are used in 400/ 230 V grades only. It is cheap, easy to install, and fairly strong.
- ❖ Lead- alloy sheathed (L.A.S.) – neat and convenient for earthing, but vulnerable to damage.

- Mineral- insulated copper sheathed (M.I.C.S.) – very strong, will withstand extremes of heat, moistures, and fumes, etc; fairly expensive.
- Aluminium – light and stiff, self supporting on bends.
- Polyvynyl chloride (P.V.C.)- these cables resist successfully the action of acid, alkali ultraviolet radiations, ozone, sun etc and are Very flexible and waterproof. These are very difficult to ignite. These wires are made in both 400 /230 V and 1100/ 600 V grades.
- V.I.R cable- in V.I.R. cable, vulcanized rubber insulation is applied over tinned copper wires to prevent attack of sulphur in the vulcanized rubber over bare copper. Although vulcanized rubber is relatively strong, it is further covered with cotton tape with braiding spun on its top. The cable is then dipped in the solutions of bitumen or wax to make it moisture proof. These wires are made in both 400 /230 V and 1100/ 600 V grades. These wires are used in casing capping and conduit wiring.

More strength and permanent protection for the cable is provided by dusts and conduits.

Ducts, consisting of shallow tubes or channels in the concrete, can be incorporated in the floors of a building at the construction stage.

Steel conduit can be either light – gauge or heavy – gauge. Light gauge, with joints clipped together, is cheap but not very reliable from the point of view of earthing

Heavy- gauge, with screwed joints, is strong, easy to re-wire, and has good earthing qualities.

Plastic or fibre conduit can also be used. It should be firmly fixed to give rigidity and usually requires a separate earth – continuity wire.

Conduits can be fixed to the surface of walls, floors or ceilings, or buried in plaster or other finishing material. Because of its poor appearance, surface fixing is not recommended for the public parts of a hotel building.

Ducts and conduits have junction boxes at intervals to enable the electric cable to the inserted or withdrawn as required, thus facilitating repairs.

Flexible wiring is normally used for lamp pendants, portable apparatus, and, temporarily, for other purposes. It is, however, only lightly protected and must not be used for permanent fixed wiring. It is considered bad practice to have flex permanently alive and apparatus should be disconnected when not in use. In addition to being protected from physical damage, a wiring system must contain safeguards against causing fire or shock. Fire is usually the result of a long period of overheating, due to overloading, a loose connection, faulty equipment, ineffective insulation, or damaged flex.

ELECTRIC CIRCUITS AND TYPES OF CIRCUITS

Electric Circuit is path of an electric current. The term is usually taken to mean a continuous path composed of conductors and conducting devices and including a source of electromotive force that drives the current around the circuit. A circuit of this type is termed a closed circuit.

Open circuit in which the current path is not continuous or current flow is interrupted is called an open circuit.

A short circuit is a closed circuit in which a direct connection is made, with no appreciable resistance, inductance, or capacitance, between the terminals of the source of electromotive force. No serious damage is likely to be done beyond the blowing a fuse.

Testing of circuits: The insulation of circuits should be tested periodically at double the normal voltage. Tests may be carried out by hand-driven generator and a direct-reading ohmmeter. The effectiveness of earthing should be tested by an earth-fault loop impedance tester of the current –injection type.

Series and parallel connection/ circuit and their applications

A series circuit is one in which the devices or elements of the circuit are arranged in such a way that the entire current (I) passes through each element without division or branching into parallel circuits.

When two or more resistances are in series in a circuit, the total resistance may be calculated by adding the values of such resistances.

$$R = r1 + r2 + r3 \ldots$$

If the resistances are in parallel, the total value of the resistance in the circuit is given by the formula:

$$\frac{1}{R_{total}} = \frac{1}{R_1} + \frac{1}{R_2} + \frac{1}{R_3} + \ldots$$

In a parallel circuit, electrical devices, such as incandescent lamps or the cells of a battery, are arranged to allow all positive (+) poles, electrodes, and terminals to be joined to one conductor, and all negative (-) ones to another conductor, so that each unit is, in effect, on a parallel branch. The value of two equal resistances in parallel is equal to half the value of the component resistances, and in every case the value of resistances in parallel is less than the value of the smallest of the individual resistances involved. In AC circuits, or circuits with varying currents, circuit components other than resistance must be considered.

FUSES

Fuses are provided at every distribution board. They take the form of a short piece of thin wire which melts or blows, thus disconnecting the supply, if the current load becomes too heavy.

There are two types:

(A) Rewirable fuses: In these fuses a length of wire is screwed to a porcelain carrier; blown fuses are repaired by replacing the wire, which should be properly secured under the washer or screw head. Kit- kat type of fuse is most commonly used fuse device in domestic installation. It consists of porcelain base which has fixed contacts to which arc is connected incoming and outgoing cables of live wire. The carrier of porcelain carries the fuse element. The main advantage of this design in the case of replacement of fuse wire which does not involve the danger of coming in contact with live parts. It is also very cheap to replace fuse wire. It, however, suffers from unreliable operation due to oxidation or due to the use of improper size of wire element. These fuses have lower rupturing capacity and, therefore, are not employed in circuit whose fault current exceeds 4 K.A. Therefore, for power circuits rewireable fuses are being replaced by HRC fuses.

(B) Cartridge fuses are self contained units with the link wire bedded in unburnable powder; they cannot be repaired; they usually give a visual indication when blown. Cartridge fuses are safer, as they smother the arc that is momentarily formed when the circuit breaks. H.R.C. fuses consists of outer ceramic body, sealed at both ends by metallic caps. To these caps are welded a number of silver wires in parallel. The space surrounding these wires is filled with compacted quartz sand which acts as a quenching medium. To the end caps are fixed tags for the purpose of fixing the fuses.

Advantages of H.R.C. fuse over rewireable fuses

1. H.R.C. fuses can successfully deal with high currents up to 46 Kamp. as against 4 Kamp. in case of rewireable fuses.
2. There is no oxidation in H.R.C. fuses due to their hermetic sealing of silver element within fuse by cementing and soldering of end caps, while rewireable fuses face the problem of oxidation.
3. H.R.C. fuse give better overload protection as compared to rewireable fuses.
4. On severe short circuits, fault current in case of H.R.C. fuse is interrupted well with in first quarter of cycle, with the result that value of short circuit current does not reach its maximum value. In rewireable fuses short circuit current is interrupted only after few

cycles. Thus, in H.R.C. fuse, both thermal and magnetic stresses on the equipment protected are reduced.

5. H.R.C. fuse is not susceptible to tampering and over fusing as rewireable fuse.
6. H.R.C. fuse has low temperature operation in comparison to kit-kat type fuse.

Circuit breakers consist of an electro-magnetic trip which breaks the circuit automatically when there is an overloading of, or a defect in, the circuit. They can be reset by hand to restore the current. If, however, the fault persists; an automatic device prevents resetting until the cause of the trouble has been remedied. Circuit breakers can be used either in place of fuses or for the earth –continuity circuit in buildings where it is difficult to obtain an effective earth connection.

A fuse must have the same current rating as the circuit it protests. It is most dangerous to replace a fuse with one of a higher rating. By preventing the fuse from blowing when there is a fault in the circuit, this may cause an outbreak of fire or the risk of an electric shock. No attempt should be made to mend a fuse until the current has been switched off. If a fuse blows again immediately after being repaired, it indicates that the apparatus, rather than the circuit, is at fault.

Causes of Blown Fuse

1. too many appliances plugged into a circuit: a 3-Kw geyser, 1 Kw electric water boiler and 750 watt house hold iron is plugged into a power circuit 15 A; Voltage 220 .

To find current flowing through the three appliances:

W = V XA

A = W/V

= 4750/ 220 = 21.59

Therefore current = 21.59 amperes.

Therefore a greater amount of current than 15 A is flowing, and consequently fuse will blow and the circuit will be broken.

2. Plugging a power appliance into a lighting circuit: e.g. A 3 Kw geyser plugged into a circuit to designed to carry 5 ampers, voltage 220.

Current flow = W/V

3000/220 = 13.63 amperes

Therefore current 13.63 amperes.

Therefore the fuse will blow. It may also cause a strain on flex.

3. Short circuit due to insulation failure

It means that lead and return wires touch and therefore current does not reach the appliance. Often due to wear of wire insulation.

Repair of Fuses

- Turn off the main switch.
- Find the fuse that has blown. This may be known before hand, if not, try each one in turn.
- Remove broken fuse wire.
- Replace with new fuse wire of the correct rating (5,10, 15 or 30 amperes).
- Before replacing the repaired fuse and before switching on, find the cause of old fuse wire melting; check all connections and the leads of the appliances if it caused the fuse is blow.

EARTHING

The risk of shock can arise from damage to insulation, the presence of water, or the working looses a connection. Electricity always takes the path of least resistance to the earth. It will therefore pass through the body of a person who is in effective contact with the earth, e.g. by touching a metal pipe or stone floor.

However, if there is an easier path to earth (e.g. a copper pipe) the current will take that in preference to passing through the human body. Protection against shock can therefore be given by ensuring that every circuit has an energy pat to earth (known as earth – continuity circuit), which will conduct harmlessly away any leaking electricity.

There are two types of earthing: In metal conduit installation, the path to earth is the conduit itself, which must be carefully laid to ensure that there is no break in its electrical continuity.

In metal–sheated cables, the path is usually metal sheath. Cables with a rubber or other insulated sheath usually have a special conductor incorporated in the core. The earth end of the circuit is attached to the water main or the metal covering of electric service cable. The circuit protects the whole of the wiring and fixed appliances, together with portable appliances if a three–pin plug is used.

As per Indian Electricity Rules No. 61 (3), all the metallic casings which are liable to be touched by hand have to be earthed.

ACCESSORIES

Switch

Switch is manually operated device for closing, opening or changing the connection in a circuit. Switches used in house wiring are of surface or tumbler type and flush type. Surface or tumbler type switches project out of the switch board and are most commonly used. Flush switches as name indicates, are flush with switch board. Flush switches are some time also called as piano switches or tiny switches. These switches, for lighting circuits are of 5 amps. Rating and for power circuits these are of 15 amp. Rating. One way switches have two terminals and are connected in series with the points. Two way switches have four terminals two of them are connected inside. These switches are used in controlling one point from two places such as in stair case wiring,. It should be clarified here that both one way and two way switches are inserted always in the live. Two pole switches are actually two single way switches linked together which control both live and neutral wires simultaneously. These switches are used as main switches for domestic installations.

In addition to above main types of switches , there are push button switches used for electric bells, table lamp and bed on-off switches. Last two types of switches have knobs of fluorescent material which enable them two glows at night.

Ceiling Roses

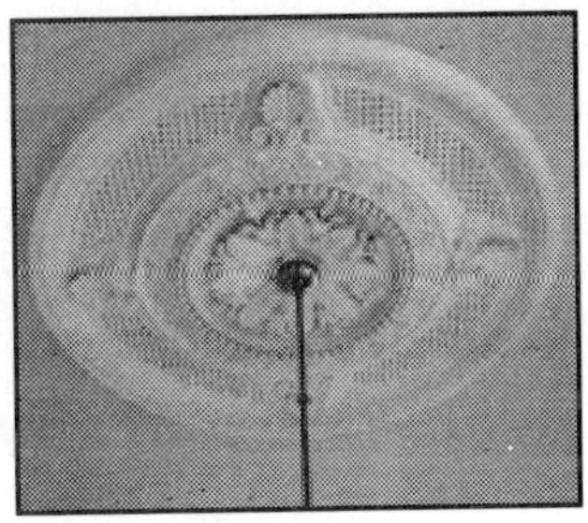

Ceiling rose forms the tapping point from electrical installation for supplying power to fans, pendants or tube lights by means of flexible cords. Ceiling roses are not used on circuit the voltage of which normally exceeds 250 V. normally only one flexible cord is attached to a ceiling rose. Ceiling roses are normally two plate type. However, three plate types of ceiling roses are used in the system of wiring employing twin cables.

Lamp Holders

Lamp holder connects the filament lamps to the electrical installation. These may be of brass or bakelite type. Latter type lamp holders do not give any shock but are less durable as compared to former type. Lamp holders for lamps upto 150 W are of Bayonet type and for lamps of 150 W and above are of Edison screw type. Edison screw type holder has centre contact which is connected to the live wire and outer or screw contact is connected to the neutral wire. Bayonet lamp holders may be pendant type, bracket type or batten holder straight type or batten holder angle type. Pendant holders are provided with cord grips. Filament lamps are hung at a height or not less than 2.5m above floor level.

Socket Outlets and Plug Tops

Portable appliances are connected to electrical installation by means of these. These may be surface type of flush type. Two pin type sockets and plug tops are used for feeding portable appliances having al insulated body such as garden standard lamp. For feeding portable appliance having metallic body it becomes necessary to earth the metallic body which ensures safety to operating personnel. Socket outlet and plug top for feeding such appliances have necessarily to be one of three pin type. Two pins are of equal size. These are connected to live and neutral wire. The third pin is thicker and longer than other two pins and is connected to earth wire in case of any leakage from the element of appliance to the metallic body; heavy current will flow through earth wire. Thicker earth pin provides sufficient contact area with hollow contact of socket. Longer earth pin engages with earth before conducting pins engage with live wire while plug top is inserted in the socket. Similarly earth pin disengages last while plug top is taken out of socket. In case of earth fault, heavy current can flow through it without over heating or burning the contact. Thicker size of earth pin also does not allow wrong insertion of three pin plug top. Usually three core flexible cords is used to connect the plug top to the appliance-green wire being used for earth pin and red and black wires for live and neutral respectively. All the plug tops are provided with cord grips and rubber brushes at their outlet. Socket outlet and plug tops are of 5 A rating for fans, table lamps, radios etc. and 15 A for power appliances such as heaters, iron etc. Every socket outlet has to be controlled by a switch fixed preferably adjacent to it. Socket outlet will be fixed at any convenient place 23 cm. above floor level.

Appliance Connectors

These are used for giving supply to household appliances such as heaters, toaster, iron press, electric kettle etc. These may have either side entry or straight entry and may be flat or round type. Twin nickel spring contacts are provided on outside to establish earth connection with the metallic body of the appliance.

Fans

Ceiling fans should be hung at not loss than 2.75 m above floor. Lead in wires will be of normal cross sectional area not less than 1.25 mm square. Fan canopies on the top and bottom of suspension rod will effectively hide the suspension and connection to the fan motor respectively. Fan must be hung by means of suspension rod from ceiling having rubber type insulator in between the two. There shall be no joint in the suspension rod as far as possible. Exhaust fans are fixed to the wall by means of rag-bolts. Connection to the fans will be by means of flexible cord taken from a ceiling rose or special connector box. Regulators are to be connected to the earth wire.

Wooden Boards and Blocks

All the ceiling roses, brackets, pendants, and accessories are to be mounted on vanished teak would blocks of depth not less than 4 cm. Similarly switches, sockets outlets and regulators etc. are mounted on teak or hard wood boards. The size of wood boards will depend upon the number of accessories to be accommodated.

TYPES OF ELECTRICAL ENERGY

Appliances and devices may require different electric-energy sources. Small buildings may have very limited electric-energy capabilities, while larger buildings (hotels, institutional buildings, and health-care facilities) may provide several electric-energy sources. In this section these sources will be briefly discussed, and management recommendations will be made for utilizing these optional resources.

DIRECT CURRENT

Direct current, or dc, has limited applications in the hospitality industry. Direct current provides a constant flow of amperes when a constant voltage is impressed on the amperes. Amperes change only if the electrical load changes or if the impressed voltage changes. Direct change is used in some security systems and for limited emergency energy use for selective devices, such as exist lighting.

For these uses, dc is probably; provided by a battery or a series of a batteries. Many data processing systems have dc sources. It is frequently important to keep theses systems in operation even when electric energy from the local electric utility is uninterrupted. These backup devices are frequently long life batteries that are automatically charged when electric energy is being supplied to the unit.

Direct current may also be generated on the property. this done only for certain types of elevator motors. Some emergency lighting systems for public areas may also operate on dc power sources. In almost all cases, a battery source will be utilized.

Alternating Current

Hospitality industry buildings are supplied with alternating current, or ac, from the local electric utility. Electric appliances and devices generally available consume ac energy.

The manager must know the characteristics of the ac being supplied to the building by the local electric utility. All electric devices used within the building must be matched to the available energy. If they are not, serious problems can result, including the loss of all electric devices.

Throughout the world a large percentage of the electrical energy used is generated by alternating current generators. It is therefore necessary to understand the principles of electricity and magnetism as they apply to alternating current.

The extensive use of alternating current has not eliminated he use of direct current. There are many applications where direct current essentially be used or it performs better than alternating current.

Applications where direct current is must or better:

- ❖ Electrochemical process: such as electroplating, refining of ores.
- ❖ For the excitation of field poles of ac generators.
- ❖ For the variable speed motors requiring precise speed control.
- ❖ For traction motors.
- ❖ For battery charging.
- ❖ For the operation of electronic equipments.
- ❖ For arc lamps used in cinema projectors and search lights.
- ❖ For some special electric welding process.

Some of the reasons for the wide use of alternating current in preference to direct current for large generating, transmission and distribution system are as follows:

- ❖ AC generators can be built in much larger power and voltage than the DC generators.
- ❖ With the alternating current, the voltage can be easily stepped up and down by means of transformers. The transformers have no moving parts to adjust or replace and the efficiency is high from 95 to 99%.
- ❖ In alternating current, long distance high voltage transmission is possible by use of step up transformer with minimum of voltage loss and line losses. Low voltage distribution is also possible by use of step down transformers.
- ❖ A.C. induction motors are simple and robust in construction, have nearly constant speed, and are smaller and cheaper than D.C. motor of equal power.

Alternating quantities: The quantities whose magnitude and direction constantly changes periodically with time are called alternating quantities

Alternating Electric Current/voltage: the electric current/voltage whose magnitude and direction continuously changes periodically with time is called alternating current/voltage.

Alternating Current: is that current, which flows with varying magnitude first in one direction and then in the reverse direction, this completes one flow-cycle or wave of constant time interval called Time period. One half of the cycle or wave is termed Positive half cycle, while the other Negative half cycle.

Various types of alternating cycles: the figures show different types of alternating cycles or waves with their respective names. These alternating current waves are used in electrical and electronic applications.

- *The alternating wave use for electric supply system*: 'Sinusoidal Wave' or 'Sine Wave' is universally employed for alternating electric supply system. The current and voltage waves are represented by the following mathematical formulas:

  $i = I_m \times \sin \Theta$

  $v = V_m \times \sin \Theta$

Where, i and v are the instantaneous values and I_m and V_m are the maximum values of current and voltage of the waves. And Theta is the time in terms of component angle value of the complete cycle of 360 degrees.

- *Sinusoidal Wave*: A sinusoidal wave is one in which the value of the quantity (emf/current induced) at any instant or time, depends upon the product of the maximum value of the quantity and the sine of the angle at that instant.
- *Wave Form*: The graphic representation of the alternating voltage or current in a circuit with respect to time is called the Waveform for the voltage or current.
- *Instantaneous value*: the value of the alternating quantity at any instant on the time line is called the instantaneous value. The value is equal to the product of the maximum value of the quantity and the sine of the angle of the required instant.
- Maximum value: the peak value of the alternating wave is known as the maximum value of the alternating quantity. It is represented by a suffix '$_{max}$' after the quantity e.g. I_{max} / V_{max}.
- Alternation: a complete set of positive values or negative values plotted against the time is known as an alternation. One alternation is equal to half cycle, since a cycle has two alternations one positive and the other negative.
- Cycle: the portion of the curve between one complete set of alternation (one each of positive and negative) and the time line is called a cycle.
- Frequency: the number of cycles of the alternating quantity per second is termed as the frequency of the quantity. It is denoted by the letter 'f' or 'n'. The unit of frequency is 'Cycles per second' and the name of the unit is 'Hertz' in short 'Hz'.
- Time Period: The time period of an alternating quantity is the time is seconds taken by the quantity to complete one full cycle.The letter 'T' denotes the time period the unit is 'second'

Relation between time period and frequency:

'T = 1 / f sec' or 'f = 1 / T'

- ❖ Average value of an alternating quantity: an alternating quantity wave has a positive and negative half cycle, which identically equal to each other. The average of the alternating quantity over a complete cycle turns out to be 'Zero'. However at times we need to calculate the average value of the alternating quantity. The average of each half of the quantity is the average of the alternating quantity.

If 'I_{av}' denotes the average value of the positive half cycle of a sine wave Alternating current, then:

$I_{av} = 2 / P \times I_{max}$ or $I_{av} = .636 \times I_{max}$.

Average Value of Alternating current: Average value of the alternating current wave is defined as the value of that direct current, which transfers the same amount of electric charge in a circuit in the same time as transferred by the alternating current in the same circuit in half time period of the cycle.

- ❖ *Root mean square value of Alternating quantity*: the power produced by a current of I amp flowing through a resistor of R ohm is $I^2 \times R$. As power is proportional to the square of the current hence power is always positive whether the value of the current is positive or negative. Energy is equal to the product of power and time ($I^2 \times R \times T$). Hence the Alternating current or voltage applied across a resistor will produce varying heat energy in both the positive and negative alternations of the cycle.
  - ❑ 'The root mean square value of an Alternating current/Voltage is given by that steady or direct current, which when flows through a circuit for a certain time produces the same amount of heat, as produced by the alternating current when flowing through the same circuit for the same time.'
  - ❑ Mathematically:

$I^2 \times R = (i_1^2 + i_2^2 + i_3^2 + ...i_n^2) \times R/n$

$I = \sqrt{[(i_1^2 + i_2^2 + i_3^2 + ...i_n^2)/n]}$

  - ❑ For a sinusoidal quantity the value of $I_{rms} = I_{max}/\sqrt{2} = I_{max} \times 0.707$
- ❖ *Form factor*: Form factor is defined as the ratio of the rms value to the average value of an alternating quantity (say current or voltage). For a wave obeying sine variation the value of the form factor is: 0.707/0.636 = 1.11.
- ❖ *Peak factor*: Peak factor of an alternating quantity is defined as the ratio of the Peak value to the RMS value.

Peak factor for sinusoidal wave = $I_{max} / I_{max} / \sqrt{2} = 1.414$.

Most hospitality industry buildings are supplied with single-phase and three-phase alternating current.

Advantages of 3-Phase system over Single Phase System

Present day generation of electrical power is almost 3-Phase; this is due to the following factors.

(i) For the transmission of given power over given distance, there is saving in the material used in conductors in 3-phase system.

(ii) For given voltage and KVA rating, electrical equipment such as alternators and transformers in 3-phase system are not only lighter, and cheaper but efficient too as compared to those in single phase system.

(iii) Magnetic flux produced due to current flow through the armature of a single phase machine is pulsating and that through the armature of a 3-phase machine is rotating one of constant magnitude. Therefore torque produced by 3-phase motors is uniform and constant whereas that produced by single phase motors is pulsating.

(iv) Single phase motors operate at very low power factor as compared to three phase motors. For the same power they draw a heavy current which produces large line losses and voltage drop in the line.

(v) Single phase motors are not self starting whereas three phase induction motors are self starting.

(vi) In 1-phase 4-wire system, we have two levels of voltage supply. Heavy loads are connected across phase wires and light loads across phase and neutral wire.

Electric Lighting

One of the primary uses of electric energy is for artificial lighting. In most buildings, lighting represents the second–highest energy use, following electric motor requirements. Light, its reflection, and object visibility are all interrelated. A light source radiates energy that you can not see. Atmospheric air is transparent to light energy, which means air does not absorb or reflect the energy passing through it. As light energy strikes a surface , it may be absorbed and converted to heat, which lowers lighting efficiency; the surface may transmit some of the energy (another energy loss); or light may be reflected than only you see reflected light.

Light colored surfaces reflect a high % of the light striking them. A black surface reflects very little light; hence, it absorbs or destroys light energy that's why it is more difficult and costly to light darker–colored than lighter colored rooms.

Light sources can also be of different colors, which produce various qualities of light. Common light sources provide "white" light, which is generation of all colors; so various objects lighted with white light appear natural or retain their real color. Red appears red when lighted with white light. Insects are yellow blind and cannot see objects lighted with yellow. Yellow to insects is like black to us. Hence, yellow light do not attract insects. Insects can see black light, which we can not see. Therefore, black light sources are used for insect traps. Some street lights for example, mercury vapor lamps- attract large numbers of insects; others, such as sodium vapor lamps, which generate tallow colors, do not appear to attract insects.

Lamp

Lamp is a source of light. A lighted candle is a lamp because it is a source of light. A lamp is inserted into a lighting fixture. The combined lamp and lighting fixture is a *luminaire.* Lamplight output is given in lumens. A lumen is a quantity of light. One very good efficiency rating for lamps is the number of lumens produced per watt of energy input.

The lumen is the amount of light energy that strikes an area at a specific distance from a standard candle. If 1 lumen falls on a 1-square foot area of a distance of 1 foot from a standard candle, it is called 1 foot-candle of light intensity; or of 1 lumen strikes 1 square meter of surface of a distance of 1 meter from a standard candle, it is called 1 lux. Foot-candles refer to the intensity of light.

Room lighting design is based on foot candle (lux) and lumens. The relationship is shown in figure. As you move farther away from the lamp, the lumens are spread over a larger surface area, so lighting intensity decreases. If correct lighting is not provided in an area, poorly lit objects can become hazards for guests as well as employees.

Lighting design depends on the foot candle (lux) intensity required at the work surface. Highly detailed work or work with high sight requirements demands high intensity light for maximum worker productivity. Hence, lighting requirements vary with the task being done. Below mentioned table shows some recommended light intensities for various tasks. These are based on extensive research and are hospitality standards.

Work area	Foot candles	Lux
Kitchen work area	30	322.8
Classrooms	40	430.4
Hotel: general areas	10	322.8
Bathroom	30	107.6
Accounting and bookkeeping	100-150	1076-1614

Food service:		
Fast food	40-50	430.4-528
Moderate-priced	#####	107.6- 215.2
High-priced	#####	53.8- 161.4

Recommended footcandle and lux intensities for selected tasks.

The kitchen work area requires 30 footcandles (322.8 lux) of light.

If the indicated amount of light is provided, worker productivity will be optimized. The lumen requirement for a 20-foot by 30 foot kitchen will be 51,500 lumens or about 32 incandescent lamps of 100 watt each.

If the same kitchen area is provided with 40 footcandles (430.4 lux) of light

The lumen requirement will be 68,495 or about 43 incandescent lamps of 100 watt each. In addition, worker productivity will decrease by from 5-10 % because of increased glare in the room.

Increased lighting cost = (43-32)/32=34.4%

In this case, the cost of energy is insignificant in comparison to the increased cost of labor.

Effects of supplying excess lighting on worker productivity

	Supply volts		
	120	110	130
Lamp voltage rating	120	120	120
Effects : Watts	100	85	115
Lumens	1600	1300	2000
Life (Hours)	1000	1500 or more	500 or less

EFFECTS OF VOLTAGE SUPPLY ON OPERATING CHARACTERISTICS OF AN INCANDESCENT LAMP

Resistance-type Lamp

Incandescent Lamps

One very common source of light which has a high-electric-resistance –filament wire. An energy flows through the filament wire, it incandesces, or glows, and the emitted energy is visible light and heat.

The lamp is available in a variety of shapes, bases and operating characteristics. The more common shapes are P (pear), PS (pear straight), and F (flame). These lamps are rated in volts, Watts, hours (life in operating hours), and lumens.

The Incandescent lamp radiates visible light that is rich in such warm colors as red, orange, and yellow. Hence, the lamps have a tendency to bring out warm reddish color of food products. Especially cooked meat and red and rose wines. You also can cut the operating cost and improve the efficiency by replacing an incandescent lamp with fluorescent lamp.

For example:

150 watt incandescent lamp may replace by 40 watt fluorescent lamp.

Installed cost of the incandescent lamp Rs. 15/-

Installed cost of the fluorescent lamp Rs. 40/-

But realizes a savings of 110 watts. Thus a lamp burns 12 hours per day the savings would be 110 watts x12 hrs per day x 365 days =481.8 KwH/year which may save your electric cost approximately Rs.2409.00 per annum think about 100 bulbs in an establishment.

Other replacements might include: 100 watt incandescent lamp with 17 watt fluorescent capsules.

60 watt bulbs with 13 watt fluorescent screw-in-types lamps.

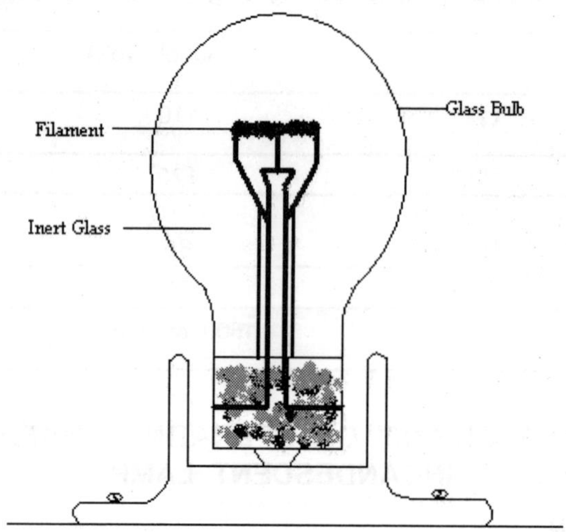

Fig. 4.1

Parts of Incandescent Electric Lamp

- *Glass bulb*: it is the thin outer cover of the lamp, commonly pear-shaped, and is made of high quality temperature resistant and shockproof clear glass. The bulb has an evacuating tip at the top, which is sealed after withdrawing the air from inside. The air is withdrawn to prevent oxidation of the metallic filament at high working temperature. The glass bulb gives firm support to other parts of the lamp and protects the internal parts. The bulbs are also designed in different other shapes for correct and desired distribution of light.

- *Glass stem*: a hollow glass stem projects inside the bulb and is fused with the top end of the glass bulb. The function of the stem is to support internal components e.g. lead-wires, a couple of filament support wires and a filament.
- *Lead wires*: the stem supports two lead wires, which come out of the glass bulb through sealed holes. At the upper end of the bulb the lead wires are soldered to the brass terminal points. The lead-wires provide a conducting path for the flow of current from the outer terminals to the filament.
- *Filament support wires*: a couple of thin steel hook wires are fixed radial to the base of the glass stem. These wires give support to the mid section of the filament so that it does not sag, vibrate or break due to heat and mechanical shock.
- *Bulb cap*: at the top of the sealed bulb, a bulb cap is fixed by adhesive cement. An insulating disc is fixed at the top of the cap and carries two brass terminals. The lead wires are soldered to these terminals. The terminals make connection with the holder terminals when the bulb is fixed; this allows the electric current to flow when the circuit is switched on. The caps are of two types:
  - *Bayonet cap*: it is a thin metallic object shaped as hollow cylinder with one end flared to fit the bulb. At the top and there are two terminals and on the curved surface there are two pins for fixing the bulb in the holder. The bulb cap is inserted in the holders with pins in the slots and then given a clockwise twist. This locks the bulb in the holder in the same way as a bayonet at the tip of a gun.
  - *Screw cap*: screws are provided on the circular surface of the metallic cap. The bulb is screwed in a special screwed holder. There is only one terminal at the top, while the metallic cap itself serves as the other terminal.
- *Filament*: it is made of tungsten, which is high resistive material and it has a high melting point (about $2{,}300^{0}$- C). When heated near to this temperature it shines brightly and gives light.

Tungsten – Halogen Lamps

Another form of resistance lamp is the tungsten- halogen, or quartz, lamp. The life of a quartz lamp is 3-4 times greater than incandescent lamp. Its efficiency equals to the most efficient incandescent lamps and its lumen output does not vary with its age; however, its initial cost is higher in comparison to an incandescent lamp; however its initial cost is higher in comparison to an incandescent lamp.

Electric Discharge Lamps

Fluorescent lamp is an electric –discharge lamp, which operates on alternating current. The operation is complex in compared to an incandescent lamp. The space between the ends is filled with low-pressure mercury gas. The electrons flowing from one end to the other are absorbed by the mercury gas, and energy is emitted- for every action there is a reaction. Now, as this different energy passes through the glass tube with its chemically coated interior, visible light energy is produced along with low temperature heat. (See Fig.4.2)

The color outputs of the lamp are variable and depend on the interior glass bulb coating. Almost every color of light can be produced. The use of warm color producing is recommended in the hospitality industries, as their color emission is similar to incandescent lamps. The life of a fluorescent is approximate 16000-25000 burning hours compared to 750-1000 burning hours of incandescent lamp. Its life efficiency decreases with age and hours of operation. The light efficiency of the lamp decreases in cold and warm temperature environments. The lamp is designed for an 26.67 degree Celsius environment. Each 10 degree Celsius reduction in environment temperature reduces the light output by almost 50% and this is the reason they take more time to start in winter season and at zero degree Fahrenheit temperature the lamp may not start without external heating. Its shapes are limited and may be in the form of straight tube, the U, and circles.

The lamp requires a special circuit for operations. Ballast is required and some lamps need a separate starter. The ballast, a wire wrapped around a piece of iron, causes an induction load, which causes volts and amperes to be out of phase; this is required for the electric-discharge effect.

The instant–start fluorescent lamp eliminates the separate starter. These lamps usually have a small diameter, making it easier to start the electric-discharge process. As the lamps do not require a starter, it is easier to maintain the circuit.

The other type of fluorescent lamp is rapid start type lamp. The cathode of this lamp is always kept hot even when the lamp is off. This is done through a special ballast technique. Although it is quickly activated but consumes energy all the time, however, the consumption of energy is less when the lamp is off.

Fluorescent lamp can be dimmed by installing electronic ballast. The electronic ballast changes alternating–current cycles, which in turn changes the light output of the lamp.

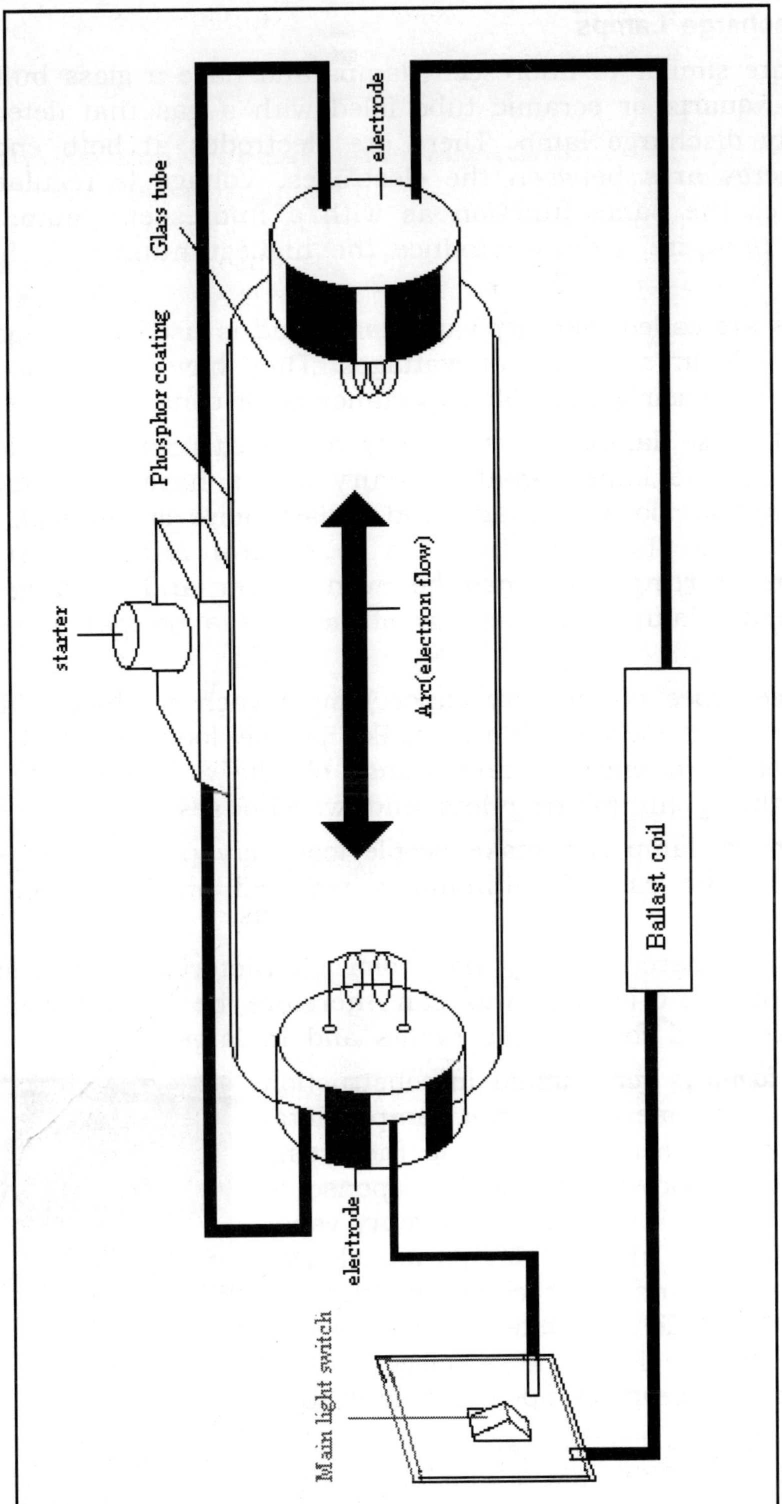
electrode
Glass tube
Phosphor coating
starter
Arc(electron flow)
Ballast coil
electrode
Main light switch

Fig.4.2

High–intensity Discharge Lamps

These lamps are similar to fluorescent lamps and have a glass bulb with an internal glass, quartz or ceramic tube filled with a gas that determines the High–intensity discharge lamp. There are electrodes at both ends the tube. Electric energy arcs between the electrodes. Voltage is regulated by ballast that serves the same function as with a fluorescent lamp. Metal halide and high pressure sodium produce the highest number of lumens per watt.

Mercury lamps are called mercury vapor lamp and is used in arcing tube. The lamps are made in a variety of wattages. They have a very long life (16000-24000 hours). Their greater life expectancy is for continuous operation.

The ballast of these lamps is very noisy and that's why it is located some distance from the lamp. Small mercury lamps have self contained ballast. These lamps are lower wattage, and ballast noise is minimal. These lamps require a long start up time (Up to several minutes). In cold temperatures, the starting time may be even longer and starting more difficult. The mercury lamp is not energy efficient as a normal fluorescent lamp.

There are three types of mercury vapor lamps; each produces different color effects. The clear mercury lamps make people look greenish. Their uses make it difficult to find red and orange objects and frequently used for large area lighting (in parking lots and warehouses).

The white mercury lamp can make people look very pale, almost sickly, with its greenish white cast. It illuminates red and orange objects very poorly.

The deluxe–white mercury lamp has color characteristics very similar to cool-white fluorescent lamps, and can therefore be used for interior lighting and mostly used for sporting events and in large exhibition areas.

Metal halide lamp is very similar in construction and operations to the mercury–vapor lamp. Metal particles are added to the mercury gas in the arcing tube. This generally improves the color response to objects, and light output is double the mercury vapor efficiency. The start time of these lamps are shorter (two to three minutes) and color characteristics fall between the white and deluxe-white mercury lamps. The Restrike time is very long and it refers to the time required to restart the lamp after it has been in operation and turned off.

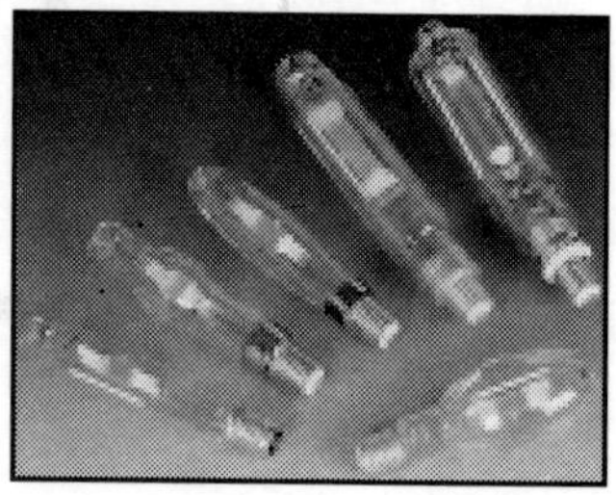

Sodium lamps have a ceramic arc tube. Sodium is the arcing gas and provides yellowish light. Their life is similar to mercury vapor lamp (16000-24000 hours) and warm-up time is similar to metal halide lamp, but its restrike time is only one-tenth of the metal halide lamp.

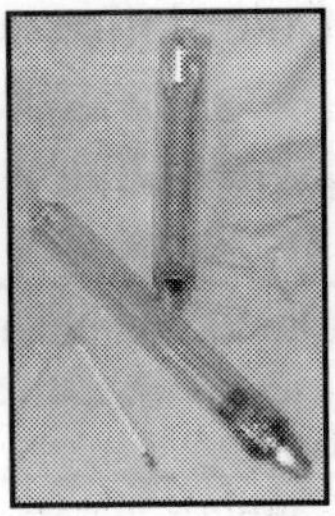

Low pressure sodium lamps (LPS), which produce about 183 lumens per watt are among the most energy –efficient light sources available. Their principal use is typically dusk-to down security lighting. However, the lamps are monochromatic, which means that they emit only one color of the spectrum. LPS might be combined with other lamp sources to produce better color rendition.

Lighting System

General uniform lighting can be provided by a variety of lighting techniques. Depending on what effects wish to create, several lighting systems are available. They are Direct, Semi direct, diffuse, semi indirect and indirect.

The most efficient lighting system is direct lighting system. All the emitted light is directed onto the activity area. This type of lighting is frequently found in institutional building because of its low installation and operating costs. Approximate 90% light goes downwards to the object and 10%light goes to the upward.

Semi direct lighting diverts a portion of the light toward the ceiling (usually less than 40%) and a larger percentage is directed downward into the activity area. The technique will highlight ceiling features and provide a soft light effect within a room and most of the board/ conference/ meeting room use this type of lighting. It is not as efficient as direct lighting system but most of the food service managers preferred it over direct lighting system.

A diffuse lighting system directs approximately equal amounts of light downward into the activity area and upward to the ceiling. This type of lighting mostly used in public area, including dining rooms and conference rooms. Cost of installation and operating is almost double in comparison to direst or semi direct lighting.

Indirect lighting reflects 90% or more of the emitted light from the luminaire to the ceiling and upper walls of the room. Therefore, light must be redirected from these surfaces down toward the activity area.

Semi indirect lighting directs between 10% to 40% of the light output directly to the activity area. These techniques are costly to install and operate for high footcandle (lux) intensities.

Generally, only direct, semi direct and diffuse lighting are recommended for large areas and rooms. The indirect and semi indirect systems are recommended only for small rooms where special effects are to be created, or where you want an especially relaxed mood, such as cocktail lounge and in guest rooms.

Calculation of Amount of Electrical Energy

a. Compute electricity bill for the month of January 2009 of ABC enterprises having the following electric load:

Electrical appliance/s	Unit Nos.	Operating Hrs/ day	Capacity
Bulbs	10	20	100 watt
Fans	10	20	60 watt
Geysers	2	2	3000 watt
Hotplate	2	2	2000 watt

b. Also calculate the capacity of fuse required.

Hints:

Electricity tariff Rs. 5/- per Kilowatt-Hour

Voltage supply: 220 volts

a. Solution for bill amount

Electrical appliance/s	Unit Nos.	Operating Hrs/ day	Capacity	Power consumption / day
Bulbs	10	20	100 watt	10 x20 x100 = 20000 watt
Fans	10	20	60 watt	10 x20 x60 = 12000 watt
Geysers	2	2	3000 watt	2 x2 x3000 = 12000 watt
Hotplate	2	2	2000 watt	2 x2 x2000 = 8000 watt
				Total 52000 watt

Capacity of fuse required = total connected load/voltage supply

A = W/V

Capacity of fuse required A= 11600/220 = 52.72 ampere

General Safety Precautions

It is our common observations that natural forces work through certain rules and regulations and abide by certain control channels. Electricity, being no exception to this, also obeys certain rules and regulations. For instance it can flow without harm and hazard if harnessed within proper barriers and channels. It is these barriers and channels which we have to know and be masters of so that the electricity works for us as our humble servant and no longer remains a life threatening and formidable monster. The other name for these barriers and channels is the safety precautions. To ensure public safety in the use of electricity. Indian Electricity Rules are laid down. These rules become applicable to every electrical installation and are mandatory in terms of Indian Electricity Act. In the following paragraphs, we will discuss certain specific provisions and practices in connection with the safe use of electricity.

1. If the live wires or electric elements are not insulated properly, this will result in not only leakage of power but it will also give shock to the persons making use of electricity. It is, therefore, necessary that insulation resistance should be above certain minimum level.
2. If the first line of defense i.e. insulation fails, we have to depend upon the second line of defense offered by earth wire and fuse. In the event of leakage being developed, the metallic body of the appliances will acquire certain potential above earth. If a human being happens to be in touch with the charges metallic body, current will flow through his body to earth.
3. All single pole switches should always be placed in live wire only and not in the neutral wire.
4. Use correct size of fuse wire. Use of over size fuses will allow isolation of the circuit only when rubber insulation of cables has been sufficiently overheated to firing temperature.
5. Many a time's too many appliances are connected to one socket outlet by means of adopter without carrying for the current carrying capacity of the wires feeding the socket outlet. This results in overloading of wires which may possibly catch fire.
6. Combustible material should not be stored near the fuse board. Spark emitted from the fuse due to short circuit and melting of the fuse element should ignite the combustible material nearby.
7. Earth wire in no case should be connected to gas pipe if any. If this is done, loose connection between the two will produce spark and gas may produce explosion.
8. Poor joints in the wiring result in minute sparking not perceptible to the eyes and hence all the connections should be periodically checked for tightness to avoid accidents.
9. Conduit wiring is safer and use P.V.C. cables.
10. In case of electrical fires, use of *carbon tetrachloride type fire extinguisher* should only be made to ensure safety. *In no case should water be thrown on the equipment and wiring to extinguish the fire.*

11. Electrical appliances should not be handled with wet hand or while standing on wet floor.
12. Insulations of wires, for connections, should be stripped off to the minimum extent necessary. If insulation is stripped off too long, the possibility of short circuit increases.
13. Electrical appliances should not be unnecessarily tampered with. Electricity does not spare any body; therefore do not take any chance with it.
14. The circuit diagram should be carefully preserved for future use. If the diagram is just printed on the equipment, it should be copied and preserved.
15. For replacing a blown fuse, main switch should first be made off.
16. Never touch naked wires unless you are sure that they are dead.
17. While working on electrical equipment, the mains should be put off and properly earthed.

SUMMARY

This chapter has considered the very basic of electrical engineering and it is not expected that students of hospitality education need to become electrical engineers but however, they must have sufficient knowledge of the subjects dealt in this topic to enable them to recognize electric faults, make the best use of modern ideas, purchases wisely, protect their own life, colleague life and most important the life of your guests who are staying or dining in your establishment by keeping a track of faulty electrical fittings and fixtures. A careful examine of your expenditure on electricity may give you an insight to perceive in better manner about your decisions. The best understanding of the topic will help you to develop in planning a safe and secure hotel or restaurant building.

Concept review questions

1. Enlist types of fuses and discuss advantages of H.R.C. fuse over rewireable fuses.
2. Describe following terms:
   1. Earthing
   2. Ampere
   3. Volt
   4. Watt
   5. Power
   6. Circuit
3. Being an owner of a catering unit how you will decide installation of wiring system.

4. Discuss types of lighting fixtures in two or three lines.
5. Explain safety precautions while handling with electric appliances.
6. Discuss types of lamps used in a small hotel building with their characteristics.
7. Discuss Advantages of 3-Phase system over Single Phase System.
8. Discuss the reasons of fuse blown off.

Numerical problems

1. (A). Compute electricity bill for the month of April 2009 of Taj enterprises having the following electric load:

Electrical appliance/s	Unit Nos.	Operating Hrs/day	Capacity
Incandescent lamps	15	10	100 watt
Hot plate dispenser	1	2	3000 watt
Rechauffe unit	1	2	2000 watt

(B). Also calculate the capacity of fuse required.

Hints:

Electricity tariff Rs. 5/- per Kilowatt-Hour

Voltage supply: 220 volts

2. A building has a load of 300 100-watt lamps. What current is required to supply the building if it is connected to 220 –volt supply?
3. Find the current flowing through a 100 watt lamp connected to 220 volt supply.
4. Three resistance of one ohm, 2 ohm and three ohm are connected in series, find equivalent resistance.
5. Three resistances of one ohm, 2 ohm and three ohm are connected in parallel, find equivalent resistance.

Project Assignments

Discuss with a chief engineer of a hotel about their installed lighting system and submit a report with its merits and demerits.

Cross examine the lighting fixtures used in your house with your colleagues.

Prepare a report on types of lighting used in your nearby areas such as your school/institute/malls/hospital/community centre and discuss with your faculty.

Examine color scheme of your model room and suggest lighting system.

5

MANAGEMENT OF REFRIGERATION AND AIR-CONDITIONING SYSTEMS

LEARNING OBJECTIVES

By the end of the lesson you will be able to:

- Define Refrigeration
- Explain types of refrigeration cycles
- Explain types of air-conditioning systems used in hotel and catering industry
- Explain care and maintenance of refrigerator and air-conditioners
- Explain energy management practices and techniques

INTRODUCTION

This chapter deals with removal of heat, or refrigeration. Refrigeration system is a need of hour not only in home but also in all types of catering units and hotels. We can not assume a life without refrigeration and air-conditioning system. Refrigeration is necessary for food storage and air-conditioning is for comfort and most prominent facility offered in hotels, clubs, food service and health care facilities. Costs of refrigeration and air-conditioning have been increasing and many energy management techniques have been utilized to reduce these costs. These techniques and latest model of refrigeration and air-conditioning are highlighted in the topic.

REFRIGERATION AND AIR CONDITIONING TERMINOLOGY

Heat Flow

Heat always flow from a warmer to a cooler substance. Heat causes some solids to become liquids or gases.

Cold

It means low temperature or lack of heat. It is the result of removing heat.

Absolute Zero Temperature

It is that temperature where molecular motion stops. It shows that there is no more heat in the substance at this point.

Pressure

Pressure is the force per unit area, and it is expressed in pascals (pa) and in kilopasaclas (Kpa).

Pascal's Law

It states that: pressure applied upon a confined fluid is transmitted equally in all directions. It is the basis of most hydraulic and pneumatic systems.

Humidity

The word humidity refers to water vapour or moisture in the air. **Air** absorbs moisture (water vapour). The amount depends on the pressure and temperature of the air. The higher the temperature of the air, the more moisture it will absorb. The higher the pressure of the air, the smaller amount of moisture it will absorb. A relative humidity of 50% indicates the air has 50% as much as it will hold at that particular temperature and pressure.

Area Measurement

The measurement of area involves the measurement of two dimensional spaces.

For example: if width of a table top is 20 cm and length of the table is 30 cm then area of the table top is 20 × 30 = 600 square cm.

Volume Measurement

The measurement of area involves the measurement of three dimensional spaces (cubic). The volume of an object is determined by multiplying the width by the length by the height.

Evaporator

It absorbs heat and must be located in the space that is to be cooled. It can maintain temperature as low as the boiling point of the refrigerant.

Compressor

There are two purpose of compressor:

1. to pump the refrigerant gas out of the evaporator
2. to increase refrigerant pressure.

Condenser

The purpose of condenser is to release the refrigerant heat that was absorbed in the evaporator and during compression.

Expansion Valve

It is primary system control and activates the compressor. When the valve allows refrigerant to flow into the evaporator, it permits the compressor to operate; when the valve closes, it stops the compressor.

Tons of Refrigeration

A ton of refrigeration represents the rate of cooling when a ton (approximately 907 Kgm or 2 000 lb) of ice melts during one 24-hour day.

1 ton = 907 Kg

Latent heat = 337 kJ/Kg

Energy absorbed = latent heat x weight

= 337 kJ/Kg × 907 Kg

= 305 659 kJ

The melting of this ice in one day has a cooling or refrigeration capacity of 305 659 kJ.

To convert the rating to a kilowatts:1 Kw = 1 Kj/sec

1 ton refrigeration capacity

= 305659/(24 × 3600 sec)

= 305659 / 86 400 sec

= 3.54 Kj/sec

= 3.54 kW

Ambient Temperature

It means the temperature of the air surrounding a motor, a control mechanism, or any other device. It is not usually constant and may change day to day and hour by hour, depending on sunshine, space and many other factors.

Critical Temperature

The critical temperature of a substance is the highest temperature at which the substance may be liquefied, regardless of the pressure allpied upon it. The condensing temperature for a refrigerant must be kept below its critical temperature. Otherwise, the refrigerator will not operate.

Refrigerants

In refrigerating systems fluids which absorb heat inside the cabinet and release it outside are called refrigerants. *These fluids, in their liquid form, under a pressure, absorb heat in the evaporator and, in absorbing heat, change to a vapour form, the fluids are taken into the compressor where the temperature and pressure are increased. This allows the heat that was absorbed in the evaporator to be released in the condenser, and the refrigerant is returned to a liquid form.* These are the members of halocarbon family and are non-toxic, no corrosive, nonexclusive, and non-flammable. Refrigerants have a relatively low specific volume. Some popular refrigerant applications are shown in table 14,1. One type of refrigerant may be used in a number of applications.

Table 5.1

Application	Refrigerants
Domestic refrigerator	R-12, R-22
Domestic food freezers	R-12, R-22. R-502
Automobile air conditioning	R-12
Home air conditioning	R-22, R-500
Public building air conditioning	
Low capacity	R-12, R-22
Medium capacity	R-11, R-12, R-22
High capacity	R-11, R-12, R-22
Frozen food delivery system	R-22., Solid carbon dioxide

Properties of Good Refrigerants

- It should be non-poisonous and non-irritant.
- It should be non-inflammable and there should be no fire or explosion hazard.
- It should be chemically stable and should not dissociate in extremes of temperature and pressure.
- It should be non-corrosive, should not react with the working pars of the compressor, evaporator and radiator.
- It should have no objectionable odour.
- Could be easily and reliably detected in case of leakage.
- The latent heat of vaporization be large to minimize the quantity of refrigerant.
- The volume of vapour for a given weight should be low to reduce the size of the compressor.
- The cost should be low.

Dry ice

Solid carbon dioxide is used for refrigeration. It is a white crystalline substance; it is formed when liquid carbon dioxide is allowed to escape into a snow chamber. It has a greater heat-absorbing capacity than water ice. Never place dry ice in a sealed container. At ordinary temperatures, the dry ice will turn into a vapour (sublime), the resulting may cause the container to explode. Avoid touching dry ice. It will instantly freeze the skin.

STUDY OF REFRIGERATION SYSTEMS

Refrigeration

- We know that heat flows from the body of higher temperature towards the low temperature body.
- Extracting heat from a body or space and transferring it somewhere else will cool or lower the temperature of the desired body or space.
- Refrigeration is the process of cooling by extraction or pumping heat out of a body or space and transferring it to another with higher heat capacity.

Methods of Natural Cooling or Refrigeration

- *Conduction*: a body is cooled by extraction of heat though conduction mode on keeping it in contact with another conducting body of lower temperature.
- *Convection*: A hot body is cooled when surrounded by a cool fluid. The cool fluids absorb and displace the heat away from the body by convection currents, thus the body looses heat and cools down.
- *Radiation*: a hot body when kept isolated in an evacuated cool space will continuously loose heat and gets cooled neither by conduction or convection but by a process known as Radiation.
- *Evaporation*: when a liquid evaporates it cools down on account of extraction of the latent heat of evaporation from its own mass and as result of this it gets cooled till the evaporation process continues, subsequently it can cool any object kept in contact with the evaporating liquid.
- *By dissolving salts*: certain salts (ammonium chloride or ammonium nitrate) when dissolved in water the temperature of the solution is lowered. The cool solution in turn will cool the object in contact with it.
- C*hemical reaction*: certain chemical reactions are endothermic, and are able to extract heat from the surrounding and lower the temperature.

- *Cooling by refrigeration*: refrigeration is a cyclic process of extracting heat out of a closed space and transferring the heat to a space of higher temperature. The method depends on the absorption of the latent heat of evaporation of a working fluid. The vapours are then compressed and allowed to loose heat in a the warmer space and get condensed the condensed fluid is again used to absorb heat by evaporation and the cycle of operation is repeated.

Basic Refrigeration Cycles

Two systems of refrigeration are common in use:

- Vapour absorption system: this system does not involve any mechanical system. It cools a space by directly using the heat of an external source. The use of electricity for heating is optional.
- Vapour compression system: it is based on the electro mechanical process; the use of a compressor is essential.

Working of the Vapour Absorption System

It functions on the principle of vapour absorption **principle.** It consists of a highly concentrated water solution of ammonia or lithium bromide gas, which acts as the cooling medium or refrigerant. When the concentrated solution is heated the gas is liberated at high pressure. The high-pressure gas on cooling in the radiator liquefies into high-pressure liquid. The high-pressure liquid refrigerant is sprayed in the evaporating chamber. The sprayed refrigerant absorbs the latent heat of evaporation in the cooling chamber. After cooling, the low-pressure gas is reabsorbed in the leftover weak solution and turns into concentrated solution to repeat the cycle.

As already told it does not contain any mechanical moving parts. The heating arrangement need not be electrical; a wick type lamp may be used as the heat source. (See Fig 5.2)

- It basically consists of the following sections and working stages:
  - *Generator*: it is a strong tank, which contains the highly concentrated solution of refrigerant. On heating the concentrated solution, refrigerant gas is liberated at high pressure. The weak solution is diverted and collected in the weak solution reservoir.
  - *Radiator*: the high-pressure refrigerant gas (ammonia) is directed to the radiator, where it looses its' heat and changes to high pressure liquid refrigerant.
  - The liquefied high-pressure refrigerant is directed to the cooling chamber where it is sprayed. The liquid refrigerant spray readily evaporates and in the process it absorbs its latent heat of vaporization, necessary for change of state. As a consequence of

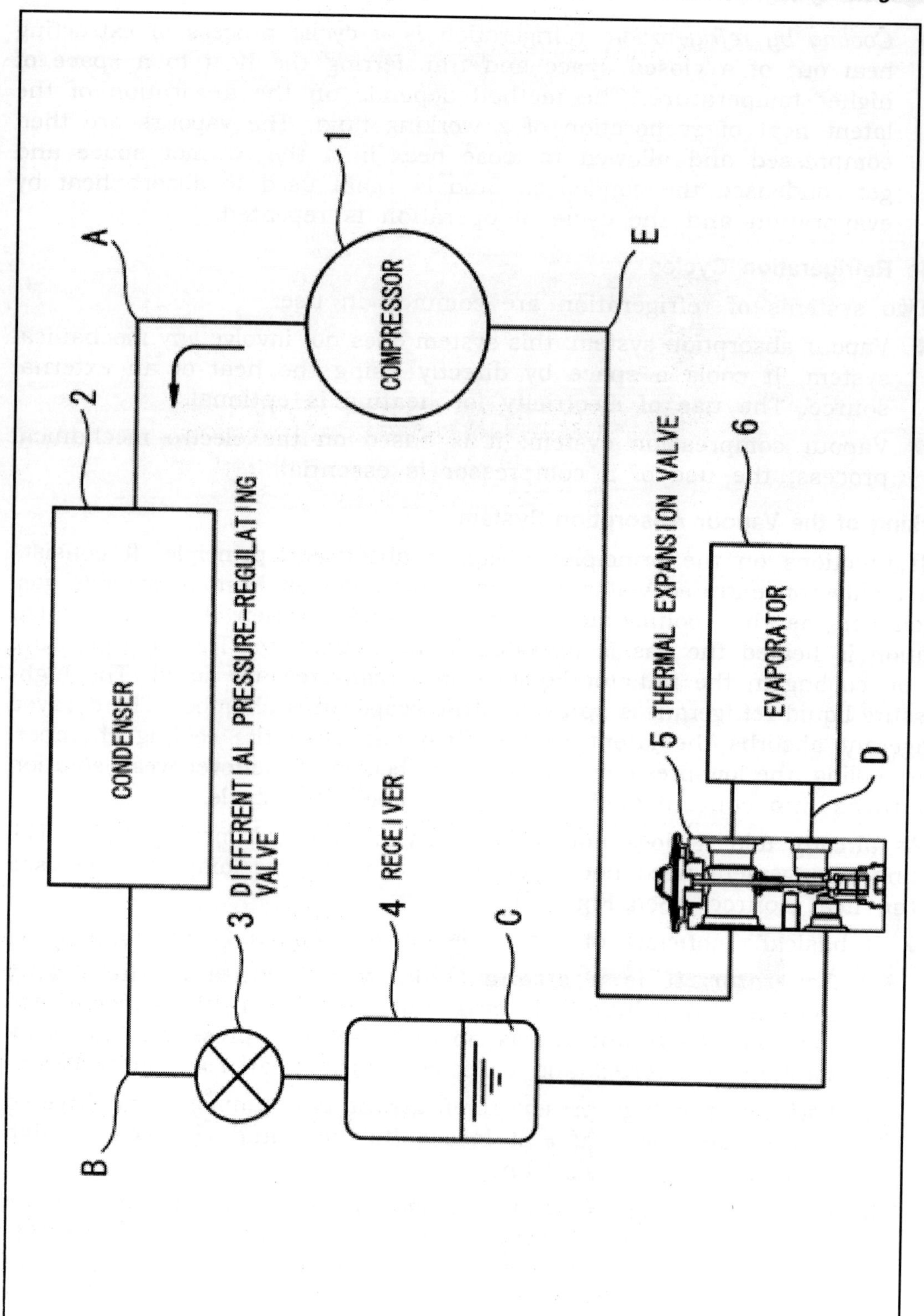

Basic Refrigeration Cycles

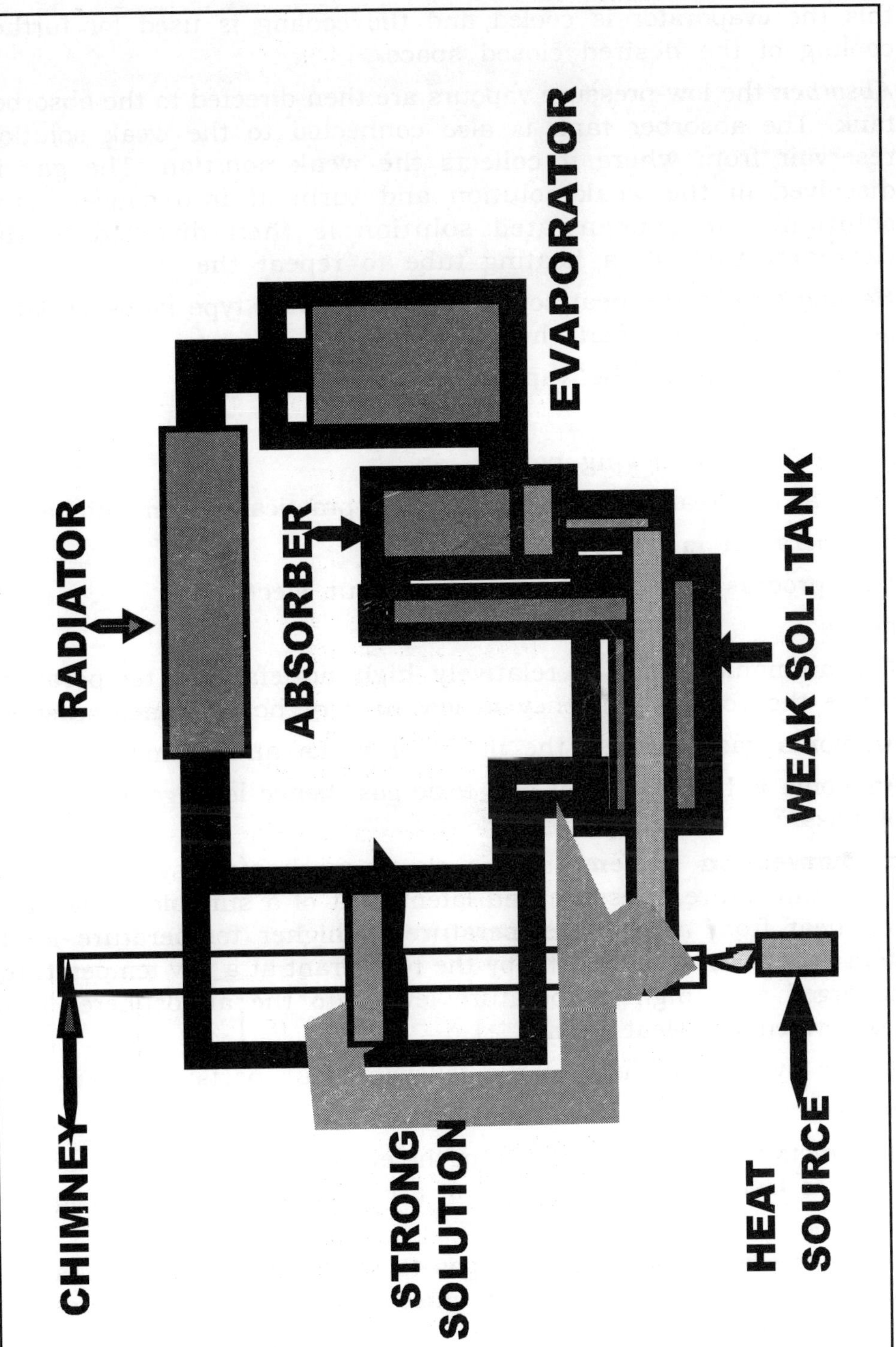

Fig. 5.2: Absorption System of Refrigeration

this the evaporator is cooled and the cooling is used for further cooling of the desired closed space.

- *Absorber*: the low-pressure vapours are then directed to the absorber tank. The absorber tank is also connected to the weak solution reservoir from where it collects the weak solution. The gas is dissolved in the weak solution and turns it into concentrated solution. The concentrated solution is then directed to the Generator through a heating tube to repeat the cycle.
- *Heating source*: the heat source may be a wick type kerosene lamp or an electric filament heater.

Merits and de-merits of the vapour absorption system:

- Merits:
  - No mechanical moving parts.
  - No wear and tear problem and requires practically no maintenance.
  - Its operation is completely silent.
  - This process can function even without electricity.
- Demerits:
  - The ammonia gas has relatively high liquefaction temperature hence the cooling efficiency is low in very hot summer seasons.
  - Ammonia gas corrodes the metal of tanks and piping.
  - Ammonia is highly irritant and toxic gas; hence leakage is a source of hazard.

Vapour compression system: this is electro-mechanical system, which makes use of temperature, pressure and latent heat of a suitable refrigerant, for pumping heat from a lower temperature to higher temperature level. In this system heat is absorbed by the by the refrigerant at a low temperature, and is discharged at a high temperature level into the atmosphere. That is why it is termed as 'Heat pump'.

Basically the system consists of the following four parts: (See Fig 5.3)

- *Compressor*: It has two fold function:
  - It extracts the refrigerant gas from the evaporator or cooling chamber coils, as fast as they are formed at a low-pressure of 35 lbs/square inch.
  - It compresses and delivers the gas to the condenser at a pressure of about 136 lbs/square inch. Because of the rapid high compression the gas becomes hot.
  - The high-pressure gas is diverted to the radiator tube.

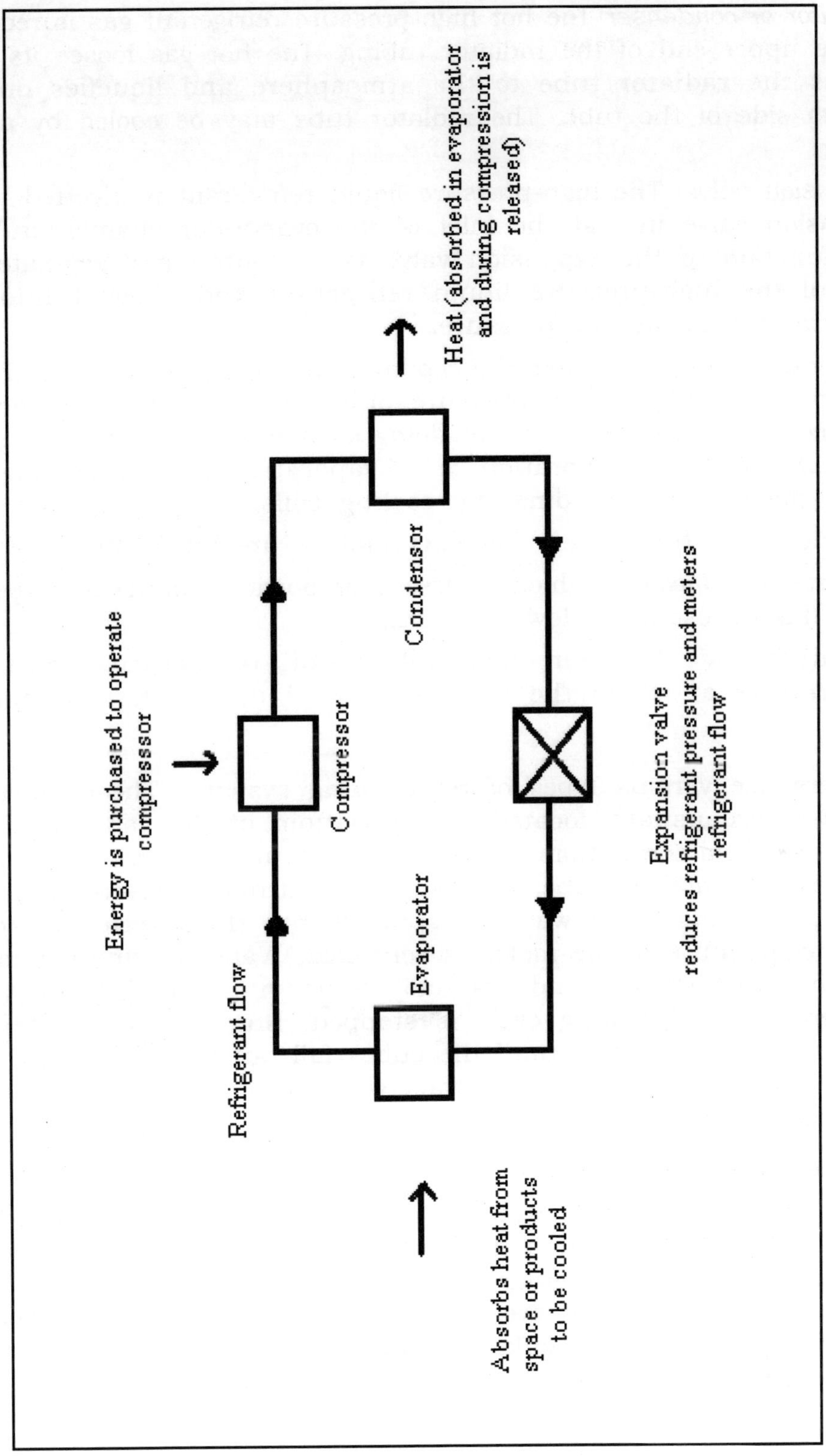
Energy is purchased to operate compresssor
Compressor
Condensor
Heat (absorbed in evaporator and during compression is released)
Expansion valve reduces refrigerant pressure and meters refrigerant flow
Evaporator
Refrigerant flow
Absorbs heat from space or products to be cooled

Fig 5.3

- *Radiator or condenser:* the hot high-pressure refrigerant gas is received at the upper end of the radiator tubing. The hot gas looses its heat across the radiator tube to the atmosphere and liquefies on the bottom side of the tube. The radiator tube may be cooled by air or water.
- *Expansion valve:* The high-pressure liquid refrigerant is diverted to an expansion valve just at the inlet of the evaporator chamber tubing. The function of the expansion valve is to control and regulate the flow of the high-pressure liquid refrigerant and allow it into the evaporator tube at low pressure.
- *Evaporator:* This constitutes the cooling unit, in which the liquid Freon (refrigerant) under a low pressure of about 35 lbs/square inch is sprayed in the cooling tubes. In doing so it quickly absorbs its quota of latent heat of evaporation and evaporates, thereby cooling the space medium surrounding the cooling coils.

The efficiency of the system depends mainly upon two factors:

- *Compression efficiency*: which is directly proportional to the compression ratio (high-pressure / low pressure)?
- The difference between the cooling coil temperature and the temperature at which the heat is rejected out of the radiator.

Ice Maker

Ice makers use various types of refrigerating systems. The compressor and condenser are usually located in the bottom of the cabinet. Liquid refrigerant flows from the bottom of the condenser up through a filter drier. It enters through a capillary tube. The evaporator surrounds inverted (upside-down) ice cube molds. Clod water is sprayed into the inverted ice cube molds. The temperature of the molds is very cold. Water striking the molds freezes to the mold surface and gradually builds up until ice cubes are formed. Then the refrigerating cycle is stopped. Now an electric heating unit heats the ice cube molds until the cubes fall out and slide down into the ice cube bin. Most surfaces in contact with water and ice are stainless steel for cleanliness.

Drinking Water Cooler

The water cooler is a special use of a refrigerating mechanism. It is used to cool water "on tap" at a drinking fountain. Since the demand on a drinking fountain is very irregular, it is necessary that it have some hold-over capacity. Still it must not over cool the water. The necessity capacity is provided by using either an insulated storage tank or large cooling surfaces in the evaporator.

The mechanism's efficiency, the waste water flows down a tube alongside or attached to the fresh water inlet. In this way, the warmer fresh water is cooled; to some extent. A water pressure regulator adjusts the bubbler. Water leaving the bubbler should be at 10 degree centigrade or 50 degree Fahrenheit. A thermostat with the control bulb attached to the water dispensing tube maintains the desired temperature of drinking water.

Air Conditioning System

Different types of air condition plants: according to the plant the air conditioners can be broadly divided into the following categories:

- Unit systems:
  - Window types units.
  - Floor mounted package units.
- CENTRAL plant system:
  - Full ducting system for cool and return air.
  - Ducting used only for conveying fresh air for ventilation with unit coolers installed in each room and served by a common refrigerant pipe system.
  - Chilled water system with unit coolers in each room with independent fresh air inlet.

Window type air conditioning units: are completely self contained units, with the compressor, condense, evaporator, refrigerant piping and air filter all assembled in a very compact assembly and fitted with an attractive frontage to harmonize with the interior of home or office.

- The window units are usually of half to two-tons capacity, and fitted with 230 volts motors up to 3 horse power.
- Modern tendency is to use sealed type compressor units with brazed piping system; so that it virtually eliminates the leakage of refrigerant and the unit can serve for long period with hardly any filling of gas.
- The condenser is air-cooled. The fan motor has blades on both ends, blades of one side cools the condenser, while the other blade circulates the room air over the chilled tubing.
- Adjustable dampers are provided to properly circulate the air in desired directions.
- There is provision to control the fresh air intake.
- Good quality filter pad is provided in the circulating fan suction duct and is capable of filtering micron size particles from the fresh and the circulating air.

❖ These units are fitted flush with the window on the interior. The bulk of the unit hangs on the exterior of the window with support on brackets.

❖ Merits:

- ❑ The units are easy and convenient to handle.
- ❑ A faulty unit can be conveniently replaced with a good one temporarily for repairs.
- ❑ Large number of units can be fitted in big rooms. This eliminates extensive alterations in the present building structure for fitting ducts.
- ❑ These units provide flexibility of operation. Units can be turned 'Off' or 'On' on requirement; this saves energy.
- ❑ These units are very popular for domestic and small offices.

❖ Demerits:

- ❑ These units are not suitable for large buildings.
- ❑ The installation and running cost is higher compared to centralized cooling for big buildings.
- ❑ These units require at least one wall of the room free and open to atmosphere, so that the hot air is discharged in the open.

❖ Package units: these units are functionally very similar to window models but are much bigger in size and therefore arranged at a suitable position on the floor of the conditioned space.

- ❑ These units contain all the elements for cleaning, cooling, ventilating, filtering humidification / dehumidification and throwing hot air to out side.
- ❑ For the ventilation and circulating air concealed duct connections are provided with the out side.
- ❑ The cover panels are removable making the access to machine parts convenient and maintenance and repair work easy.
- ❑ Adjustable dampers are provided to divert cool air to desired directions in the room.
- ❑ Merits:
  - ◆ Only one or two such units are sufficient for a moderately large room or hall.
  - ◆ Extensive alteration of the building is not required.
  - ◆ They are easily installed and replaced with new ones for temporary repairs.

- Units can be easily switched on and off as per requirement; thus saves energy.

❑ Demerits:

- The installation cost is higher compared to central cooling for large buildings.

❖ Central A.C. plant with air ducting: A central plant with full ducting is best suited for air conditioning of large buildings, such as theatres, halls and un-partitioned offices those having interiors which do not have an outside exposed wall. The conditioning plant consists of two or more heavy compressors including the attached essential components. These are located at central place preferably usually on the ground or basement level of the building.

❑ The conditioned air is delivered through a ducting system to all parts of the building. A duplicate ducting system is required to lead back the return air from the inside to the plant to be humidify/ de-humidify and recharged with fresh air to be circulated again.

❑ Demerits:

- The ducts are bulky, as they have to handle a large quantity of air, they occupy a lot of space.
- Poses lot of difficulties to conceal these heavy ducting and requires substantial changes in the building structure.
- Individual choice control is not possible
- It permits mixing of air, cigarette smoke, bacteria and odors between different areas and offices.

❑ Merits:

- The processing of air is centrally controlled and easy to work with.
- The efficiency of the plant is high.
- It is sturdier and operates for long periods with less attention.
- Summer load is easily taken care of.

❖ Chilled water system: this system overcomes the difficulties encountered of the above system. Water is used as the transfer medium to carry the heat absorbed in the rooms back to the central cooling plant where the water is cooled again. Individual heat exchanging units are provided in each room and chilled water is piped into the units. The cool water absorbs the room heat and is diverted back to the cooling plant.

❑ Merits:

- This is a flexible system and well suited for large and multi-storey buildings as well as for medium and small buildings.
- Heavy duct arrangement is not required.
- Checks mixing of air of different rooms.
- Permits individual control of temperature and fresh air content.
- Exchanger units are simple in design with no moving parts, silent in operation and practically maintenance free.
- The piped water conveying system is equally good for conveying hot water in winters for heating the rooms.
- Pipe work is un-obstructive and can be concealed in the building walls.
- The system is very flexible in nature i.e. exchanger units can be switched on and off as required.
- The chilled water storage tank is quite sufficient to run a few exchange units even after the cooling plant shutdown only by running the water circulation pump. This improves the economic efficiency.

❑ Demerits:

- There is some amount of heat absorption in the chilled water pipe work; this can be minimized by proper lagging (heat insulation) of the pipe work.

CARE AND MAINTENANCE

Refrigeration System

- Do not place refrigerated equipment near sources of heat or near window area where the sun's rays will strike any portion of the unit.
- Keep the condenser clean and open to allow air to circulate around it.
- Dirt accumulations on the condenser serve as insulators and reduce the rate of heat transfer from the condenser to the environment.
- Ensure periodic vacuum cleaning of air cooled condenser.
- Kitchen grease may have to be removed by washing.
- Use best quality of insulation and must have a low thermal conductivity rating.
- Serious thought should be given to increasing thickness of insulation.

Air-conditioning System

- Ensure correct ventilation system in a building.
- Air filters should be cleaned or changed at frequent intervals.
- Motor and fan bearings should be proper greased or oiled.
- Ensure insulation of ducts.
- Check interiors of the ducts periodically.
- If belt driven connections are used between the fan and motor, belt slippage must be to keep a minimum.
- An energy management system may also include ventilation control.

Energy Management Systems for Refrigeration Cycles

By introduction of computer controlled energy management system, considerable savings can be made by the owner of the property. This system continually monitors temperature of compressor, condenser, evaporator, and cooled space. As temperatures are continuously monitored in the cool areas an undesirable high temperature could activate an alarm if stored products are in potential danger. The system can control expansion devices and compressor operating times. The same system can be installed food chillers or freezer entrances by personnel. A well qualified refrigerator engineer or mechanic can quickly review temperatures and identify if a refrigeration cycle is operating efficiently. The EMS will also control performance of cooling tower and regulate the flow of water or air. A well designed and maintained computer EMS can reduce energy consumption by 20% or more, reduce the cost of spares, maintenance cost, and equipment –down time, reduce product spoilage etc.

SUMMARY

This chapter focus on the removal of heat or refrigeration system and generating comfort conditions by using different air-conditioning system. Components of the vapour–compression cycle include the evaporator, compressor, condenser an expansion valve. Most of the refrigerated units used refrigerant belongs to family of halocarbons. Students must be aware about various modes of air-conditioning so a brief about the same is given. A summary of best Techniques to conserve energy and how to maintain the refrigeration and air-conditioning system is also highlighted in the topic.

Concept Review Questions

1. Define the following terms:
   - Ambient temperature
   - Critical temperature

- ❑ Pressure
- ❑ Relative humidity
- ❑ Unit of refrigeration
- ❑ Dry ice
- ❑ refrigerants

2. Define refrigeration and basic two cycles of refrigeration.
3. Enumerate with the help of neat diagram vapour-absorption refrigeration cycle.
4. Explain types of air conditioning systems.
5. How you will care and maintain refrigeration and air-conditioning units.
6. What do you mean by EMS? Discuss its importance in refrigeration and air-conditioning systems.

Project Assignments

1. Discuss the effect of non-smoking sections, on the ventilation and air filtration requirements for the building you are going to visit.
2. Determine the type of air-conditioning systems in your local hotel building, health care, food service facilities.
3. Discuss when one would use the vapour-compression and lithium bromide absorption refrigeration cycles for cooling.
4. To what extent are plastic strip door coverings used in local food service establishments.
5. Visit a local food service unit and obtain as much information as you can on the following:

Number and sizes of refrigeration units and purpose of these systems. Determine if there are more efficient systems that could be used to replace the existing systems.

6

BUILDING TRANSPORT SYSTEM

LEARNING OBJECTIVES

By the end of the lesson you will be able to:

- Understand basic fundamentals of electrical engineering.
- Explain types of wire with their characteristics
- Explain different types of fixtures used in hotel and catering industry
- Explain single phase and three phase ac supply
- Explain types of lighting
- Calculate amount of bill incurred on electricity consumption
- Explain safety in handling clectrical equipment

INTRODUCTION

There are two types of building transport systems namely vertical and horizontal transport in buildings of more than three floors and vertical transport is more common in comparison to horizontal one and used to carry guests, employees to deliver services in the guest rooms and product movement. These systems are very complicated in terms of maintenance and require a lot of energy. This chapter deals with both types of building transport system with their care and maintenance techniques.

VERTICAL TRANSPORT TECHNIQUES

There are four techniques involved in vertical transportation namely Stairwells, Elevators, Escalators, and Gravity chutes or drops. The first three are most common in the hospitality buildings and ramps are most energy efficient techniques.

STAIRWELLS

Stairwell is a form of vertical transport system and it is essential to have stairwell in all types of building more than one floor and must be fireproofed so the guests can safely exit upper building levels. Owners have to follow local building codes and fire codes to determine the size if width and depth of the steps. Stairwells must be properly lighted and emergency lightings are required in interior stairwells if adequate natural light is not sufficient. Provision of handrails and non-slip steps are recommended for safety purpose. Stairwells are normally made of concrete and steel. Stairwells must generally exit close to a building exit door.

ELEVATORS

The term *elevator* generally denotes a unit with automatic safety devices; the very earliest units were called hoists. Elevators consist of a platform or car traveling in vertical guides in a shaft with related hoisting and lowering mechanisms and a source of power. There are two types of elevator systems used for mass movement of guests and freight. They are cable and hydraulic elevators. Cable elevators are most common because it is fast, smooth and quiet.

Cable elevator system has following parts:

1. Shaft
2. Guide rails
3. Counterweights
4. Shaft safety devices
5. Elevator car
6. Cable
7. Elevator machine

Shaft is the main part of the elevator in which elevator is positioned. Lower part of the shaft is pit and upper part is control room. If control room is located on the roof of the building, it is called pent house. Shaft is positioned from lowest level to highest level of building.

Guide rails is positioned in the shaft and elevator car moves by wheels on the guide rails.

Counterweights are arranged in the cable in such a manner so adjustment of weight can manage automatically and it varies according to size of elevator car or capacity of elevator.

Cable is a steel rope consisting of many wires and life of cable depend on miles traveled, starts and stops.

There are two types of elevator machine with cable elevator: geared traction and gearless traction machines.

The geared traction machine has an electric motor driving a series of gears. Since the gears are attached with the machine so speed is slow.

Gearless machine has a long life but heavy initial cost and can provide high car speed and very smooth ride. Figure 6.1 shows the major components of cable-elevator system.

In hydraulic elevator system, there are no counter weights and these are replaced by a plunger, which is part of elevator machine. This is only the basic difference between the two elevator systems.

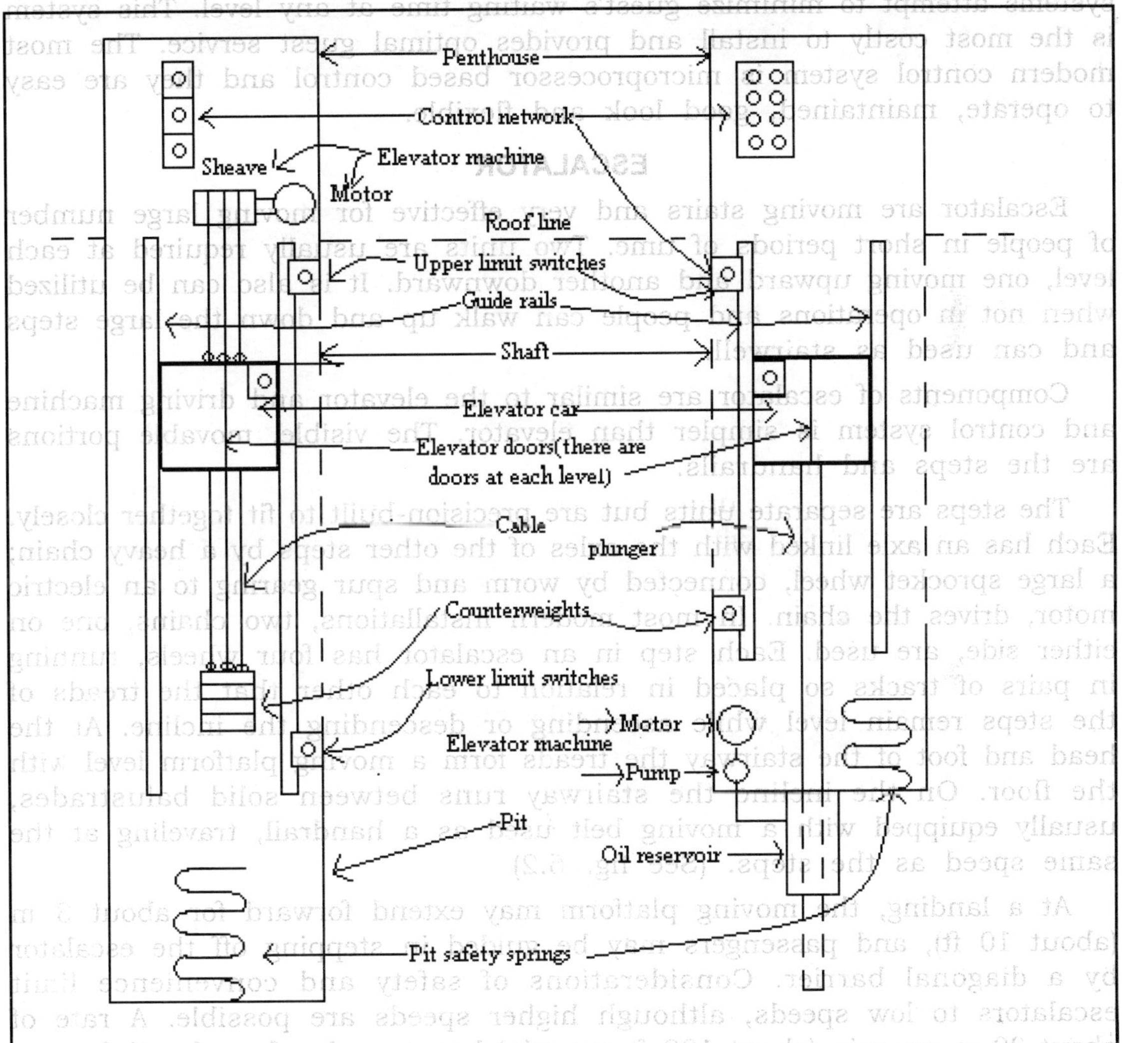

Fig. 6.1

Elevators are so well-contained that even people who use them daily may not realize how they operate. When someone pushes a button to call an available elevator on another floor, the safety doors (frequently double doors) close and an electric lifting motor switches on. The motor turns a drum, around which the cable system is wound. Counterweights are used to balance the weight of the elevator car and relieve the tension on the cables, so that when the car is going up, the weights are going down, and vice versa. A guiding rack keeps the elevator moving smoothly in the shaft, and floor buffers prevent the car from bouncing when it comes to a stop. A safety braking system (located just below the car) and touch-sensitive doors prevent potential injuries to passengers. Fully computerized control systems attempt to minimize guest's waiting time at any level. This system is the most costly to install and provides optimal guest service. The most modern control system is microprocessor based control and they are easy to operate, maintained, good look and flexible.

ESCALATOR

Escalator are moving stairs and very effective for moving large number of people in short periods of time. Two units are usually required at each level, one moving upward and another downward. It is also can be utilized when not in operations and people can walk up and down the large steps and can used as stairwell.

Components of escalator are similar to the elevator and driving machine and control system is simpler than elevator. The visible, movable portions are the steps and handrails.

The steps are separate units but are precision-built to fit together closely. Each has an axle linked with the axles of the other steps by a heavy chain; a large sprocket wheel, connected by worm and spur gearing to an electric motor, drives the chain. In most modern installations, two chains, one on either side, are used. Each step in an escalator has four wheels, running in pairs of tracks so placed in relation to each other that the treads of the steps remain level while ascending or descending the incline. At the head and foot of the stairway the treads form a moving platform level with the floor. On the incline the stairway runs between solid balustrades, usually equipped with a moving belt used as a handrail, traveling at the same speed as the steps. (See fig. 6.2)

At a landing, the moving platform may extend forward for about 3 m (about 10 ft), and passengers may be guided in stepping off the escalator by a diagonal barrier. Considerations of safety and convenience limit escalators to low speeds, although higher speeds are possible. A rate of about 30 m per min (about 100 ft per min) has proved safe and satisfactory. The carrying capacity is determined by the width of the steps, which is generally either 81 cm or 122 cm (32 in or 48 in).

Functions

Each individual step of an escalator is constructed as a carriage provided with 4 small wheels. The top and the bottom pair of the wheels each run

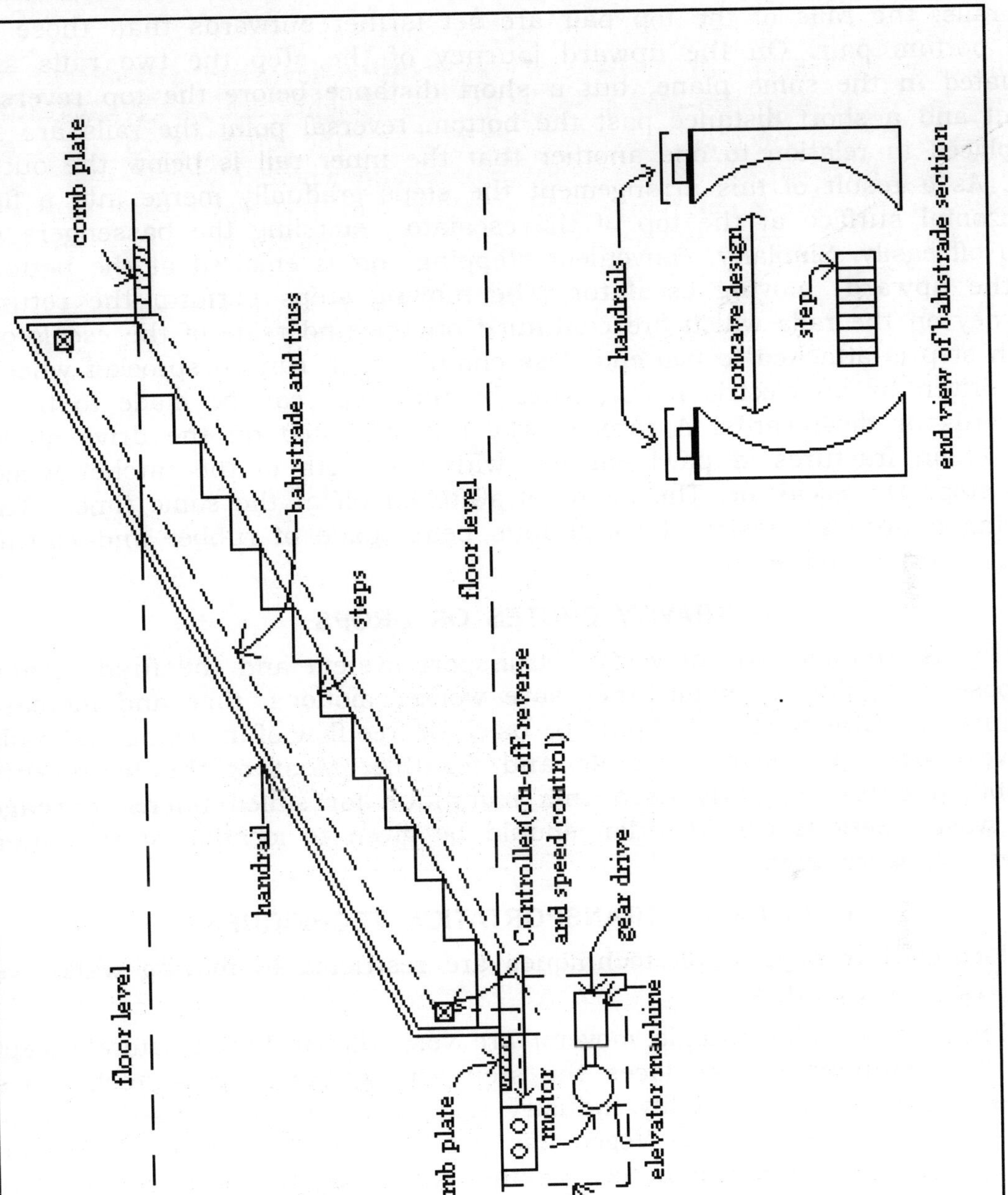
comb plate
balustrade and truss
floor level
steps
handrails
concave design
step
end view of balustrade section
handrail
Controller(on-off-reverse
and speed control)
gear drive
elevator machine
motor
comb plate
pit
floor level

Fig. 6.2

on rails; the rails of the top pair are set farther outwards than those of the bottom pair. On the upward journey of the step the two rails are situated in the same plane, but a short distance before the top reversal point and a short distance past the bottom reversal point the rails are so displaced in relation to one another that the inner rail is below the outer rail. As a result of this arrangement the steps gradually merge into a flat horizontal surface at the top of the escalator, enabling the passengers to step off easily. Similarly, convenient stepping –on is ensured at the bottom of the upward- moving escalator. The moving steps perform the return journey on the rails which are continued on the underside of the escalator. Each step is attached to two end -less chains which run on sprocket wheels are driven by an electric motor, whereby the steps can be made to travel upwards or downwards. A ratchet wheel is mounted on the drive shaft. If a chain fractures, a pawl engages with the teeth of the ratchet wheel and stops the escalator. The motor is switched off at the same time. The moving handrails consist of continuous belts made of rubber and canvas plies incorporated in it.

GRAVITY CHUTES OR DROPS

This is another type of vertical transport system and the fundamental purpose of chutes is simple: they save worker motions, time and increase productivity. Gravity chutes should be used for free flow of incoming materials to work area whenever possible and feasible. Most of the hospitality establishments frequently used this technique for soiled linens, garbage and waste. Serious consideration should be given to locating storage area above the work area.

HORIZONTAL TRANSPORTATION TECHNIQUES

Horizontal transportation techniques are restricted to moving walkways and halls or corridors.

Moving side walks (people movers) are very similar to escalators except that a continuous belt replaces the step arrangement. These techniques are not common in hospitality industry and most commonly used in large air ports. (One hotel in Las Vegas has two one way people movers which take guests only into the hotel's casino area).

Corridors are universally used as horizontal transportation techniques and width of corridor depends on the number of people and the equipment that are to move through it. If the hall has an incline, or a few steps, handrails must be provided.

Care and Maintenance

1. Shaft of the elevator provides a natural chimney with the building and must be fireproof.

2. Routine check of cable wire.
3. Schedule periodic lubrication of counterweights and plunger.
4. Routine inspection of elevators and escalators, a single accident could have adverse effect on a hospitality building for several years.
5. Follow local codes and manufacture's instruction for care and maintenance.
6. Good building layout helps in maintenance and reducing the cost on transportation system.

SUMMARY

Building transportation system is very important like other systems such as refrigeration and air conditioning, lighting system, water system and care full design and consideration. Energy management is difficult for vertical horizontal and vertical transport system but proper care and maintenance of these systems can help in reducing the operating cost.

CONCEPT REVIEW QUESTIONS

1. Explain in one or two lines:
   - ❑ Elevator cable
   - ❑ Stairwells
   - ❑ Shaft
   - ❑ Elevator machine
   - ❑ Counter weights
2. Discuss possibilities of types of vertical and horizontal transportation system in a sixteen floors five star hotel building.
3. Discuss with the help of neat diagram functioning of an elevator car.
4. Why ramps are important on lobby level. Explain.

PROJECT ASSIGNMENTS

1. Visit a five star hotel and find out types of existing transport system and discuss WITH maintenance engineer its care and maintenance program.
2. Compare transport systems find in a busy mall with a hotel building.
3. Prepare catalogue by visiting various leading suppliers and do comparative study of building transport facilities and services provided by them.

7

FIRE PREVENTION AND FIRE FIGHTING SYSTEM

LEARNING OBJECTIVES

By the end of the lesson you will be able to:

- ❖ Define fire and its causes
- ❖ Explain classes of fire
- ❖ Explain fire extinguishing techniques
- ❖ Explain types of fire detectors, and fire alarms
- ❖ Explain legal requirements
- ❖ Explain care and maintenance of fire extinguishing devices

INTRODUCTION

The Hotel Management is fully responsible for the safety and the well being of guests as well as of the hotel staff. In case of any harm to the costumer due to accidents on account of negligence, the hotel management has to face legal proceedings and pay compensation as decided by the Court of Law. Such occurrences bring a bad name to the organization and affect business. The management must pay serious attention for the personal safety and security of the guests, customers, patients, members of organization and building property. The management should understand the importance of remaining prepared for events that threaten the life and property of guests and employees, as well as the assets of the business. The common problems generally center on:

- ❖ Fire.
- ❖ Accidents in the hotel e.g. Electrical-shock, burning, injury due to falling or slipping and swimming pool accidents.
- ❖ To some extent on natural disasters e.g. earthquakes, floods and tornadoes.

❖ Criminal attacks on guest and the theft of guest and hotel properties.

Terminology

Combustion and burning: are essentially oxidation processes in which a material known as fuel combines with oxygen with the release of energies (heat, light, pressure and sound) and production of its oxide.

Explosion: The process in which a material oxidizes at an extremely high rate to release vast amount of heat, light, flames, pressure and sound. The vast amount of heat released in the very short period expand the released gases and the surrounding air, which in turn generate a loud sound and the high pressure damages the objects in the surrounding space.

Fire: is defined as the rapid rate of combustion with release of heat, light and flames.

Smoldering: is comparatively slow process of combustion with release of heat and light but no flames.

Rusting or Decay: is a very slow process of combustion or oxidation organic and inorganic materials accompanied with very slow evolution of heat only.

Fire

Fire is the most common damaging agent and a major disaster. About 80% of the property is rendered total loss after a building is engulfed in fire; at the same time fire causes substantial number of burn and deaths cases. Provisions should be made for the safety of customers and property against fire.

Classification of Fires

According to the type of the fuels, fires can be classified under the following categories:

❖ Type 'A' fire: This type of fire is causes by burning of solid organic materials, for example wood, plastic, paper, cloth and rubber etc. Type 'A' fire is also known as 'General fire'.

❖ Type 'B' fire: caused by burning of liquid organic materials, for example petrol, diesel, kerosene oil, alcohol and other oils, cause the type of the fire. This 'B' fire is also known as 'Oil Fire'.

❖ Type 'C' fire: burning of inorganic materials causes this fire, for example Potassium, Sodium, sulfur etc. This fire is also known as 'Chemical fire'.

❖ Type 'D' fire: This fire is caused by the combustion of both organic and inorganic gases, for example Methane, petroleum gases and Hydrogen gas etc. This fire is known as 'Gaseous fires'.

❖ Type 'E' fire: Electrical sparks or short circuit initiates the fire and it is maintained by the burning of combustible materials used as indicated above. This fire is known as 'Electrical fire' and requires different preventive techniques.

The Conditions for Fire

The following three conditions are essential for starting and maintaining fire:

- ❖ Presence of combustible material or fuel.
- ❖ Presence of oxygenated air: oxygen is supporter of combustion and is essential for it. Normal air contains about 20% of oxygen of its volume.
- ❖ Ignition temperature: fuel materials have their own specific ignition temperatures. This temperature is necessary to start combustion and maintain fire.
- ❖ Variation in any one of the above conditions will affect and control the intensity of fire.
- ❖ The above condition is explained with the 'Fire triangle' diagram. The fire will maintain itself if the triangle is closed.

How a fire starts and sustains itself:

- ❖ When an external heat source heats a fuel material in the presence of oxygen, the portion of the substance, which first attains the ignition temperature, starts burning.
- ❖ The heat liberated by the combustion process is dived in two portions:
  - ❑ One part of the heat generated by burning is released to the atmosphere.
  - ❑ The other part of the heat is utilized in warming and raising the temperature of the fuel material adjoining the burning zone. Under favorable conditions if the adjoining material attains its proper ignition temperature the fire proceeds further and sustains itself.
  - ❑ If this part of heat is not enough to raise the temperature of the fuel material to the ignition point the fire will not sustain and would ultimately extinguish.
  - ❑ At the same time other fire sustaining conditions (oxygenated air and fuel material) should be available.

Conditions, which will retard or subdue fire:

- ❖ Restriction or absence of combustible material.
- ❖ Restriction or absence of oxygenated air affects the intensity of fire and under severe reduction of oxygen the fire may not be able to sustain itself.

- Coolness or less heat of fire; if the heat of the fire is not sufficient enough to raise the temperature of adjoining fuel material up to the ignition point, the fire will not sustain.

Methods for Extinguish Fires

- Methods, which depend on the cutting off the fuel:
  - Removing the un-burnt fuel material away from the vicinity of the fire. This method is not suitable for closed spaces or heavy materials objects. The shifting is difficult due to smoke in the closed space or due to the weight of the objects.
- Methods depending on the oxygen supply cut off:
  - Covering the fire with a layer of un-combustible materials will restrict air to reach the fire zone. The fire gets starved of oxygen and extinguishes. Example putting sand or dust on burning material or covering it with woolen blankets.
- Methods depending on the cooling of the fires:
  - If large amount of air is blown over small fire it absorbs the heat of the fire and the adjoining material fails to reach ignition temperature and the fire is unable to sustain itself.
  - Small explosions over the fire remove the hot gases and cool the fire by expanding the hot flames. This method is vastly used is controlling the oil well fires.
  - Pouring water over general fires: the pouring of water over the fire first absorbs the sensible heat (heat to raise its temperature to the boiling point) and secondly absorbs vast amount of heat as latent heat of vaporization. Thus the fire is cooled and quickly brought under control.

Fire Prevention Techniques

General Fires

- If conditions favor the fire can be contained in a limited space by the removal of the un-burnt fuel material from the vicinity of the fire.
- Covering the fire by a layer of incombustible material such as sand, thick woolen blanket etc. This restricts air supply and controls the fire.
- Spraying or throwing water over general fires, controls it. Water forms a temporary layer on the burning surface and restricts air supply. At the same time water absorbs sensible heat @ 1 kilocalorie per kg per degree Celsius up to boiling point and then 540 kilocalorie per kg as the latent heat of evaporation. The heat thus absorbed cools

the fire and drops the temperature much below the ignition point. Further the water vapors envelope the fire and restrict the air supply to fire. Water therefore proves to be an easily available good fire quencher for general fires.

Oil Fires

- *It should be noted that sand or water should never be used to quench oil fires.* The reasons being that sand and water are heavier than oil and settle down in the burning oil mass, leaving the top burning layer in contact with air to continue burning. At the same time the sand or water, which settles in the oil, displaces the burning oil and spreads the fire further.
- For control of oil fires foam type fire extinguisher should be used. The foam spreads on the top of the burning oil surface and cuts off the air to come in contact with it.
- Dry calcium bi-carbonate powder extinguisher can also be used with oil fires. Bicarbonate powder releases carbon dioxide gas on coming contact with the burning layer. The powder, oil and carbon dioxide gas forms foam with CO_2 filled bubbles, which floats on the surface and cuts the air supply to burning surface.

Gas Fires

- These fires require very special techniques to control them:
  - Use of oxygen absorbing gases: Some gases such as 'Halon' 1301 (bromotrifluoromethane) is especially favored for extinguishing general and gaseous fires and electrical equipments because it leaves no residue and does not cause electrical short circuits or damaging corrosion of the equipment. These gases have a very high affinity for oxygen and they absorb about 20 times of their own volume, of oxygen. When sprayed over the gas fire zone they absorb the oxygen from the space around the fire and by creating an oxygen deficient zone around it extinguish it. These chemical gases are though very costly but are very efficient not only for gaseous fires but other fires as well.
  - Explosion method: This method is suitable only for gas fires, especially in oil fields. A series of explosions are carried out in quick succession over the gas fire. The fire heat ignites the explosive material, which absorbs a large amount of oxygen from the surrounding during explosion. Simultaneously explosions create a high pressure over the space thus spreading the fire. The spreading of the fire helps to cool and control the fire. This method is highly technical and requires experienced people and sophisticated machine.

Electric Fire

- It should be noted that water or Soda acid fire extinguisher should never be used in case of electric caused fires.

  The reason is that water and soda acid extinguishers products are good conductor of electricity. This may cause spread of electric current and electrocution of the fire fighting persons.
- For attending electrical fires special carbon tetra chloride fire extinguishers are used. CCl_4, which is an insulating liquid is stored in container and sprayed with the help of pressurized Nitrogen gas. The Nitrogen gas displaces the oxygen and covers the fire and the liquid cools the fire.
- Nitrogen displaced foam type fire extinguisher may also be used in some cases of electrical fires.

Some of the important points are noted below:

- The design of the building should comply fully with the established rules and regulations of fire safety norms.
- The building structure should be so designed that the fire can be isolated and contained in the affected portions without much spreading to other portions of the building.
- The building design should be able to ventilate hot gases, smokes and toxic fumes to reduce suffocation and also the building temperature does not increase much so that the evacuation of people is made easier.
- The building design should provide enough and easy EXIT points for quick evacuation of guests and hotel staff.
- Enough emergency stairs should be provided out side the building to serve as exits in case the internal stairs are full of smoke.
- Good fire alarm system is provided in all sections of the building and especially in strategic areas such as kitchens, storerooms and underground floors.
- Enough automatic fire extinguishing systems and manually operated extinguishers are provided at suitable and easily approachable points in every section of the building.
- Large overhead and underground water storage tanks should the maintained full of water, exclusively for fire emergency.
- The readiness of fire alarm and fire extinguishing systems should be checked at scheduled intervals.
- The hotel staff should be trained to respond to fire emergency without panic and should prove helpful to the customers not much familiar with the hotel corridors and exit points.

FIRE ALARM CIRCUITS

Fire alarm is a device used to warn the occupants of a building, the presence of a fire before it spreads and blocks escape routes or attempts to extinguish it.

On sensing smoke the detectors emit a loud, high-pitched alarm tone, usually intermittent and sometimes accompanied by a flashing lights.

There are two types of smoke detector:

1. Photoelectric smoke detectors:

   ❖ *Light beam obstruction detector*: Utilize a small light source and a light-sensitive cell. The spot of light falls on the photocell; due to this the photocell generates current that keeps an alarm circuit 'open'. When particles of smoke interrupt the ray of light, the photocell stops generating current and the alarm circuit is triggered 'on'. Sometimes the control circuit is so arranged that it automatically start water-sprinkling system in the affected zone. The system is to be installed high enough so that the beam of light is not interfered by the general movement on the floor area.

   ❖ *Light diffusion smoke detector*: This photoelectric detector is widely used; it employs a detection chamber in which smoke can enter. The light and the photocell are fixed in the chamber in such a way that light-sensitive element cannot ordinarily "see" the light source, usually a light-emitting diode [LED]. When particles of smoke enters the chamber that holds both the LED and the photocell, the smoke particles diffuse or scatter the light ray so it can be "seen" by the photocell. As a result the light-sensitive cell generate a current is and the alarm is triggered. Photoelectric detectors respond faster and more effectively to the large smoke particles generated by a smoldering, slow-burning fire.

2. *Ionization detectors*: Employs radioactive material in so tiny quantities that they pose no significant health hazard. The radiation beam ionizes the air molecules between a pair of electrodes in the detection chamber. This enables a minute current to be conducted by the ionized air. When smoke enters the chamber, the smoke particles attach themselves to ions and diminish the flow of current. The reduction in current triggers 'On' the alarm circuit.

   1. Ionization detectors respond faster to the tiny smoke particles released by a rapid burning fire. For this reason some manufacturers produce combination versions of detectors. Many fire-prevention authorities recommend the use of both photoelectric and ionization types in various locations in a private home. Either type of detector.

Local rules regarding fire safety and the building design

- Provision of correct types of fire extinguishers at appropriate positions.
  - Properly designed building structure to localize and prevent spread of smoke and fire to unaffected sections of building.
  - Properly designed smoke-free staircases.
  - Enough safe escape routes for the guests and employees for quick evacuation of building.
  - Enough water in suitable capacity overhead and underground tanks for emergency water supply during fire accidents.
  - Provision of fire and smoke sensors and alarms.
  - Automatic water sprinkling arrangement at strategic positions in the hotel building.
  - Provision of staff training to handle fire situations and help costumers to get out of the building through safe and convenient routes.
  - Exit access: there should be two separate exits are required from each floor or area of the building.
  - Distance a guest or employees should have to travel before reaching an exit should be according to NFPA.(National Fire Protection Act).
  - Doors must swing open to outside.
  - Discharge area should be clear and not blocked by vehicles, debris or other material.
  - The exit should be illuminated on a continual basis.
  - Emergency power should be arranged so as to provide the required illumination automatically in the event of any interruption of normal lighting. All lighted exit signs should also be connected to the emergency power supply.
  - Follow the local codes (NFPA) which generally specify the size of letters, color, lighting level and position of sign.

General Accidents

Arrangement should be made for the safety of the costumers and staff:

- Electrical safety norms should be strictly adhered according to rules in force.
- Electrical control and safety devices such as switch, fuse and 'earth' etc. should be provided and tested at regular intervals.
- Staff should be trained to handle electrical shock accidents and fires caused by electricity.

- To prevent general accidents the building floor should be kept clean of slippery materials e.g. oil, soap, high polish and wax etc.
- The floors of passages and movement areas should be free of obstructions.
- Staircase side rails should be strong and properly fixed.
- Hanging and overhead machines and equipments should be properly fixed on ceiling and walls at proper height as not to obstruct movement.
- Rotating machines should be properly guarded.
- Strong and well-fixed grills should be provided in the windows to prevent accidental falling and attempted suicidal jumping.
- Swimming pool rules and safety precaution should be strictly observed.
- Trained guides should be available at the swimming pool during swimming sessions.
- Some beds in a well-established hospital should be kept hired for necessary emergency admission of hotel patients.
- A well-equipped ambulance van with staff must be maintained by the hotel round the clock to transfer the patient to hospital without delay.

Natural Disasters

Are though rare but when they strike they create havoc. Their occurrence and effect can neither be ruled out nor predicted, but the damage can no doubt be minimized if proper preventive measures are ensured.

The management must ensure that the local safety rules and regulations presently in force for such disasters are strictly observed without any discrepancies whatsoever.

Hotel management should be in touch with the local authorities for advance warnings, help and rescue facilities.

Criminal cases are very common in hotels. The guests, customers and employees of the hospitality industry are vulnerable to robbery, assault, rape and larceny. The management should seriously consider the effectiveness of security personnel, procedures and equipments. The following information will focus on desirable practices and equipment that decrease the likelihood of crime.

Restricted Access many lodging units and other related hospitality activities allow unrestricted entry and movement of visitors everywhere in the building. This results in the approaches and main building to remain open 24 hours a day. Poor security of the perimeters and the building can create potentially hazardous situations for the safety of guests and property. The criminals do generally carry out their activities in the buildings and the lodging areas.

Restricted access has a psychological effect on an offender. It signals a warning that steps have been taken to check them. At the same time it generates confidence in the customers that steps are in force to protect them.

- ❖ Closed circuit television monitoring of the hotel floors, galleries, urinals and stairs is a must.
  - ❑ *Lighting*: A dimly lit area provides favorable conditions for criminal activities not only against the guests and costumers but also guests' and building properties. On the other hand a well-lit area is a psychological deterrent to criminal activities.
- ❖ The best checking time of exterior building lighting is dark late evening hours. The checking during dark late hour gives the actual lighting conditions and discrepancies of the present scheme.
- ❖ Extra fill up lights should be installed for deficient light positions to cover the dark zones and improve illumination.
- ❖ The lighting system should be electronically controlled and self-activating. It should automatically switch on and off with changes in natural light levels.

Parking

Vehicle-parking facilities need constant watch and monitoring to minimize:

- ❖ Exhaust pollution in the parking area.
- ❖ Proper parking of vehicles.
- ❖ Risks of hit and run accidents.
- ❖ Vandalism.
- ❖ Auto-theft, and burglaries in the parking area.
- ❖ Pollution and security of the parking area will improve if the management:
  - ❑ Provides displacement arrangement (ventilation) of the vehicle exhaust gases with fresh air in the parking zone.
  - ❑ Utilizes the services of uniformed vigilance staff.
  - ❑ Provides adequate lighting in the area.
  - ❑ Provides CCTV to monitor the parking areas.
- ❖ To reduce the incidence of room theft and assaults in the high rise buildings with inter-connecting section and galleries, all persons entering the building from the garage areas should pass through manned and monitored security posts or through supervised lobby or electronic security devices before they can enter the guest area.

- ❖ Problems occur when people can enter unnoticed in an elevator in the garage area and travel and roam unnoticed and unchecked at a floor in the building.
- ❖ Constant CCTV monitoring should be provided at strategic points in the elevators, lobbies and galleries.

Doors Locks and Windows

Consider the following guidelines:

- ❖ Solid-core doors should preferably be used on the corridors or exterior openings. The average hollow-core wood or iron doorframe can be easily punched through even the doors are provided with strong locks.
- ❖ Hinges on all guest room doors should be concealed. An intruder can easily snap off exposed hinges with simple tools.
- ❖ Strong metal doorframes should be used for guest rooms. Wooden or hollow metal frame can be peeled off or twisted to render the doors useless.
- ❖ Dead-bolt latches and locks are to be provided on guest-room doors. The bolt must extend at least 1 inch (25.4 mm) from the door lock into a bolt receptacle in the doorframe. The lock must automatically engage when the door is closed so that the room occupant does not have to bother to engage the lock.
- ❖ Spy lens must be provided on the doors at face level.
- ❖ Coded or computerized locks should be used instead of keyed locks. These locks allow the guest to program their own codes on a plastic card. In case of loss or theft of the card the code needs to be changed by the hotel computer system.
- ❖ Strong grills or special burglary resistance glass panes should be provided on the windows.

Key Control

Locks are useless with out correct key control arrangement.

- ❖ The security manger should ensure that the keys to guest rooms are unmarked and should not identify the room location in the property.
- ❖ The keys should be stamped with the massage "DO NOT DUPLICATE" and should be changed only when a key loss is reported.
- ❖ Keys should be available to the room-service workers on a controlled and recorded basis. The records should mention the name of the room-service worker, time of issue and return of the key.
- ❖ Coded and computerized locks provide greater protection and key control.

- Different types of card systems are in use to mark the personal identity number (PIN) by the guests.

- *Valuables*: Since problems can occur with key and control of codes, the manager may have to provide a 'property safe' (locker room) at the front desk, some other secure area or the guest rooms itself for the protection of expensive property. The safe should have the following specifications:
  - Safes should be fire resistant and should be able to protect the valuables inside for specified time at the specified temperature.
  - The safes should have burglary resistant rating.
  - They should be firmly secured in the building structure as not to be easily removed and stolen together with the contents inside.
  - Should have easy re-coding facility with new occupancy of room.

Safety Measures in Mechanical Workshops and Electrical Installations

1. The following safety precautions should be taken in workshops where mechanical work is undertaken:
   - Unauthorized persons should not be allowed to enter the workshop and operate any machine.
   - All the exterior moving and rotating parts of machines such as belts and pulleys should be guarded with a cover.
   - Proper eye protecting glasses and hand gloves should be worn while grinding and welding.
   - Shoes with Hard heels and toes should be worn in workshops.
   - Properly fitting clothes be worn. Neckties and other loose clothes should be strictly avoided.
   - Helmets should always be used in workshops.
   - Tight Apron should be worn over the normal clothes.
   - All the sections of machines, which carry electrical current or voltage should be well guard covered with an enclosure.
   - All load lifting tools and tackles such as chain pulley blocks and cranes should be mechanically strong and tested at proper intervals according to rule. The test records are properly maintained for inspection by factory inspectors.
   - Proper clearance should be provided between machines and between machine and workshop walls for easy movement and maintenance.
   - Machines should not be over speeded beyond the rated limit.
   - Machine should not be overloaded beyond the rated capacity.

- ❑ While handling explosive and combustible materials proper protection should be undertaken.
- ❑ While handling corrosive chemicals proper eye and body protection be undertaken.
- ❑ Oil should not be spoilt on the floor to prevent slipping and if it is there it should be properly cleaned immediately.
- ❑ Danger boards and indicating light should be installed at proper places so that they are easily visible.
- ❑ Vulcanized rubber mats should be used under the feet while operating a machine run by electrical energy.
- ❑ Recommended fire extinguishers should be fixed at strategic places and should be easily approachable.
- ❑ Workers should be trained to operate and attend to machines under their responsibility.
- ❑ The workshop should be properly ventilated.
- ❑ The work place should be properly illuminated.
- ❑ The working place should be maintained neat and clean.
- ❑ All the tools should be flawless and in good working condition.

SUMMARY

Safety and security nowadays are a top priority of hospitality industry. Protecting the lives and valuables of guests, employees, suppliers, is a fundamental duty of the hotel management. Various safety and security procedures adopted by the industry and norms of National Fire Protection Act are discussed in the topic.

CONCEPT REVIEW QUESTIONS

- ❑ Why should the management bother about safety of guests in their hotel?
- ❑ What are the common unsafe conditions for which you will give a thought as a manager of a hotel?
- ❑ Classify fire and recommend procedures for extinguishing.
- ❑ Prepare a write up how you will ensure safe and secure conditions in mechanical workshop.
- ❑ Why staff training is necessary for safety and security of hotel building.

PROJECT ASSIGNMENTS

- ❑ Visit a five star hotel and prepare a project on guest safety and security.

- Do the comparative analysis of safety and security procedures adopted in a catering unit with club facilities.
- Determine the extent to which life safety is, or has been, a problem in the following types of facilities in your city:

  a. Hotel

  b. Food service

  c. Health-care

  d. Club

  e. Institutional buildings

8

WASTE DISPOSAL AND POLLUTION CONTROL

LEARNING OBJECTIVES

By the end of the lesson you will be able to:

- Define pollution
- Explain types of pollution
- Explain techniques adopted to control pollution
- Explain legal requirements for hotel and catering industry
- Explain types of waste in hotel and catering industry
- Explain practices and techniques used to control waste

INTRODUCTION

A hotel is a mini 'Ecosystem' (world) in itself and generates quite enough waste materials during its daily operation. To prevent a dirty look and polluted conditions these wastes are to be taken care of and properly disposed. It is a better and cheaper proposition to dispose the wastes through the local municipal department. If the facility is not available, the hotel management has to make its own arrangements to dispose the wastes. Great responsibility lies on the hotel management to make disposal of the different waste materials effective, flaw proof and safe, so that exterior environment is not polluted. The waste disposal arrangement includes program for the collection of the wastes from the different departments of hotel to a common collection point and then to dispose the different wastes by the best practical methods in accordance with the local environment and health rules.

Pollution, contamination of Earth's environment with materials that interfere with human health, the quality of life, or the natural functioning of *ecosystems* (living organisms and their physical surroundings). Although some environmental pollution is a result of natural causes such as volcanic eruptions, most is caused by human activities.

There are two main categories of polluting materials, or pollutants. Biodegradable pollutants are materials, such as sewage, that rapidly decompose by natural processes. These pollutants become a problem when added to the environment faster than they can decompose (*see* Sewage Disposal). Non-degradable pollutants are materials that either do not decompose or decompose slowly in the natural environment. Once contamination occurs, it is difficult or impossible to remove these pollutants from the environment.

Non-degradable compounds such as dichlorodiphenyltrichloroethane (DDT), dioxins, polychlorinated biphenyls (PCBs), and radioactive materials can reach dangerous levels of accumulation as they are passed up the food chain into the bodies of progressively larger animals. For example, molecules of toxic compounds may collect on the surface of aquatic plants without doing much damage to the plants. A small fish that grazes on these plants accumulates a high concentration of the toxin. Larger fish or other carnivores that eat the small fish will accumulate even greater, and possibly life-threatening, concentrations of the compound. This process is known as bioaccumulation.

Definition of Pollution

Pollution is the introduction of unwanted, usually harmful material in the environment. A pollutant is the material that harms the environment. Unfortunately, almost all pollution such as water, air, and land has been caused by human activities.

Impacts of Pollution

Depletion of ozone layer

The protective layer in the atmosphere that shields Earth from the Sun's harmful ultraviolet rays.

Cost of pollution control itself a major impact of pollution. Millions of rupees are spending by Government and industries to control the pollution and which can be spend on betterment and up gradation of infrastructure, facilities and services.

Social implication Research has shown that low-income populations and minorities do not receive the same protection from environmental contamination as do higher-income communities. Toxic waste incinerators, chemical plants, and solid waste dumps are often located in low-income communities because of a lack of organized, informed community involvement in municipal decision-making processes.

Pollution exists in many forms and affects many different aspects of Earth's environment such as acid rain, green house effect and global warming.

Point-source pollution comes from specific, localized, and identifiable sources, such as sewage pipelines or industrial smokestacks.

Non-point-source pollution comes from dispersed or uncontained sources, such as contaminated water runoff from urban areas or automobile emissions.

The effects of these pollutants may be immediate or delayed. Primary effects of pollution occur immediately after contamination occurs, such as the death of marine plants and wildlife after an oil spill at sea.

Secondary effects may be delayed or may persist in the environment into the future, perhaps going unnoticed for many years. DDT, a non-degradable compound, seldom poisons birds immediately, but gradually accumulates in their bodies.

Types of pollution:

1. Air Pollution
2. Water Pollution
3. Sound Pollution
4. Solid Waste Pollution

Air Pollution

Presence of harmful gases and solid particles in air leads to air pollution. It is increasing in big cities very rapidly and has an not only adverse effect on human beings but also on other animals and plants too.

Causes of Air Pollution

1. By burning of fossil fuels in power houses, industries and vehicles. This gives off gases, such as Carbon monoxide, Sulphur dioxide and Nitrogen dioxide.
2. Sulphur dioxide is formed when coal that contains sulphur is burned. This gas is also present in car exhaust. When it combines with oxygen and water in the air forms sulphuric acid. The mixture of acid and rainwater that falls on the earth is called *acid rain.*
3. Increasing volume of carbon dioxide is major cause of deforestation.

Effects of Air pollution

1. It causes irritation of eyes, dizziness, headache and respiratory diseases like bronchitis and asthma.
2. Pollutants like lead released from the exhaust engines when inhaled cause damage of liver and reproductive organs.
3. Excess carbon dioxide in the atmosphere traps the heat of Sun leading to rise in the temperature of the earth over a period of time. This is called *Greenhouse effect.* The increasing in temperature of the earth

cal lead to melting of polar ice caps resulting in flood in coastal regions.

4. *Acid rain* corrodes metals and damages marble. Taj Mahal, a beautiful heritage monument made up of marble has been affected by acid rain. Acid rain is also responsible for death of many aquatic animals. It also affects soil fertility by making the soil acidic. Plants do not survive in acidic soil.

> Urban air pollution is commonly known as smog. The dark London smog that Evelyn wrote of is generally a smoky mixture of carbon monoxide and organic compounds from incomplete combustion (burning) of fossil fuels such as coal, and sulfur dioxide from impurities in the fuels. As the smog ages and reacts with oxygen, organic and sulfuric acids condense as droplets, increasing the haze. Smog developed into a major health hazard by the 20th century. In 1948, 19 people died and thousands were sickened by smog in the small U.S. steel-mill town of Donora, Pennsylvania. In 1952, about 4,000 Londoners died of its effects.
>
> One of the greatest challenges caused by air pollution is global warming, an increase in Earth's temperature due to the buildup of certain atmospheric gases such as carbon dioxide. With the heavy use of fossil fuels in the 20th century, atmospheric concentrations of carbon dioxide have risen dramatically. Carbon dioxide and other gases, known as greenhouse gases, reduce the escape of heat from the planet without blocking radiation coming from the Sun. Because of this greenhouse effect, average global temperatures are expected to rise 1.4 to 5.8 Celsius degrees (2.5 to 10.4 Fahrenheit degrees) by the year 2100. Although this trend appears to be a small change, the increase would make the Earth warmer than it has been in the last 125,000 years, possibly changing climate patterns, affecting crop production, disrupting wildlife distributions, and raising the sea level.

Control of Air Pollution

- Pollution check certificate to be obtained after every three months by the owners of cars, scooters, etc.
- Use of CNG as fuel for buses instead of diesel in all the states.
- Use of unleaded petrol.
- Use of car pools by office goers and school children.
- Use of bicycle for short distance traveling within the colony.
- Shifting of industrial units from residential areas to industrial areas which are far away from the cities.

- ❖ Industries to treat the gases released from the chimney.
- ❖ Changing the energy source from fossil fuel based to renewable energy based like solar power, wind power or biogas.
- ❖ Use of pollution control equipment e.g. fabric filters, wet scrubber and electrostatic precipitators.
- ❖ Creating awareness and education of the masses.
- ❖ Laws need to be more strict and better. There are some laws that help curb air pollution in our country. The environment (protection) Act, 1986, and the Air (prevention and control of pollution) Act, 1981, are some of the Laws that curb air pollution in our country.
- ❖ Research work on improved technology: hotel industry must conduct research and find better eco-friendly technology that reduces pollution. We are already working on solar power and many other such technologies that reduce pollution.
- ❖ Setting emission standards: it is another good way of controlling air pollution. Standards are set by mostly pollution control boards or laws that define the amount to which an industry can emit pollutants. If emission is more then legal action is taken. There are emission standards for automobiles too. Some of them are Euro norms and Bharat norms.

Water pollution

Water pollution refers to the presence of harmful material in water. We all tend to take clean water for granted but in many places in the world, clean water is already in short supply due to water pollution. Pollution makes water unsafe for drinking, washing, cooking and sometimes even for recreation. At times it is so polluted that it is unfit even for irrigation.

Causes of Air Pollution

- ❖ When untreated sewage (waste water from sinks, showers, and toilets) is released into rivers, it is broken down by bacteria. The bacteria use oxygen in this process. When large amounts of sewage are dumped, the oxygen in water decreases. As a result, fish and other living organisms in water may die from lack of oxygen.
- ❖ Industries often release waste into rivers. The waste released contains certain metals which are harmful for living organisms.
- ❖ Excessive use of fertilizers and pesticides cause water pollution sine they are carried to water sources with rainwater.
- ❖ Throwing of dead animals and dumping of other solid wastes into water.
- ❖ Excessive use of detergents.

- Bathing and washing of clothes by human beings in ponds and rivers.
- Human beings and animals defecating in or near water sources.
- Oil spills from oil tankers in the ocean kill fish, mollusks, water birds, and other marine animals.
- Power plants use cold water from lakes or rivers to cool heated machines. The heated water is then returned to the lakes and rivers. Even small change in temperature can kill many living organisms in water.

Effects of Water Pollution

- Polluted water can cause serious water-borne diseases like typhoid, jaundice, dysentery and cholera.
- It destroys aquatic plants and animals.
- Because of the pollutants quality of water goes down. It leads to abnormal growth of plants and may lead to death of flora and fauna.
- Many pollutants released from industries seriously affect human being: mercury damages nervous system, cadmium, a heavy metal, makes bone fragile. Pesticides can cause cancer and affects our immune system.

Control of Water Pollution

- Chemical waste released by factories should be treated before releasing into rivers.
- Sewage water should be treated before being released.
- Prohibition of throwing of dead bodies of animals in water bodies.
- Creating awareness amongst masses about the importance of clean water.
- Stronger and better enforced regulation/ legislation: laws need to be made more strict and better. The environment (protection) Act, 1986, and the Water (prevention and control of pollution) Act, 1974are some of the Laws that curb water pollution in our country.
- Reducing fertilizer and pesticides usage in agricultural fields.

Noise Pollution

Understanding Noise

- In acoustics, noise means any undesired sound, which is irritant and objectionable or, which interferes with other intelligible sounds that are being listened to.
- Noises are random (unpredictable and unsystematic) and undesirable sound signals, which produce an unpleasant hearing effect and at the same time mask the desired intelligible sound signals.

- In a simple way, Noise is the unwanted and or unpleasant sounds, which masks (covers) the intelligible sounds and makes hearing difficult.

Types of Noise

- White noise: In music, the effect of the complete range of audible sound wave frequencies heard simultaneously (at the same time), analogous to white light, which contains all the frequencies of the light spectrum seen simultaneously. The sounds of cymbals and big drums have white noise characteristics. White noise is a-periodic sound of un-uniform wave pattern of constituent frequencies are of random amplitude and occur at random intervals.
- Its detrimental effects are on the increase day by day. The increase of industries, types and number of transport vehicles and advances in information and entertainment technologies has added further to the natural noise sources.
- Due to the above reasons noise is present in every walk of our lives:
  - Home.
  - Workplace.
  - During travel on roads.
  - During the leisure activities.

Sources of noise: the sources of noise can be divided in two categories:

- Natural: any sound created by natural sources which disturb hearing e.g. sound of big streams, waterfalls, storm, animal noises etc.
- Artificial: any noise created by manmade sources or machines such as :

Exterior Sources

- Transport:
  - Roads: due to different type of transport modes and transport generated noise.
  - Air: planes and helicopters.
  - Water: steamers and powerboats.
  - Rail transport: trains, subway trains and trams etc.
- Construction:
  - Of big buildings.
  - Sport stadiums
- Industry:
  - Depends on the type, location and process of the industry.

Interior Sources

- Equipments and systems fixed in the building.
  - Air conditioners and air conditioning plants.
  - Ventilation systems.
  - Exhaust fans.
  - Compressors.
  - Lifts and elevators.
  - Ice machines.
  - Laundry machines.

Modes of Entertainment

- Open areas: music groups, games, function areas: public gathering and revelry.
- Covered areas: discos, theatres, feasts and public gathering.

Effects of noise on the environment: noise affects the bio-world to a large extent. It casts its detrimental effect both on the animal and plant world. It impedes the growth of the plant world, while it very adversely affects the animal world specially the humans who are already under lot of stress. Some of the bad effects are listed below.

- **Human health**
  - o Retards the process of growth.
  - o Induces High blood pressure (hyper tension).
  - o Affects the digestive process and promote chances ulcers.
  - o Damage to the hearing system. Noises at 60 db become unbearable while noises of 120 db may cause permanent deafness.
  - o Circulatory disturbances: palpitation, breathlessness and dizziness.
  - o Neurasthenia: weakness of the nerves and mental disorders.
  - o Nervous breakdown.
  - o Induces irritation and aggressiveness.
  - o Insomnia or sleeplessness.
  - o Induces General fatigue with lack of motivation, feeling of inadequacy and bad moods.
- **Privacy.**
- **Disturbed environment:**
  - Communication.
  - Difficulty in concentration

Measure of Noise

The loudness of sounds noise is measured in logarithmic units known as decibels (db) while the intensity is measured in watts per square m (watts/m^2). Every 100-fold increase in the sound intensity level actually represents an increase of one bell (ten decibels) in the loudness. Unit of sound level intensity (Loudness) is bell, named after Alexander Graham Bell; defined as $\log_{10}$ (L/Lo), where L is the sound level intensity in question and Lo is defined as 10^{-12}W/m2, roughly equal to the faintest audible sound; a decibel is a tenth of a bell. A selection of the common sound levels is given in the following table:

1	Jet Aircraft	120 db
2	Heavy Machinery	90 db
3	Busy Street	70 db
4	Conversation	50 db
5	Whisper	20 db

Difference between Intensity of sound and Loudness: While the intensity is the actual measure of force per unit area created by a sound signal, Loudness is the level of sensation by a person. To explain this a sound signal may be very loud for a small baby, it is normally loud for an adult while it may be very feeble for an old man with impaired hearing.

To explain the difference mathematically while one baby is crying, we shall sense some loudness with that intensity. Now if ten babies are crying the intensity will increase ten fold but the loudness will increase by one level or logarithm of ten or 1db. Similarly when 100 babies will cry together the intensity will increase 100 fold but the sound loudness will be 10 times of the original one baby or 1 bel.

Sensitivity to sound: Sensitivity to sound depends on:

- Age.
- Sex.
- Present health condition.
- Present stress condition.
- Time of the day.
- Present activity.
- Acoustic factors.

Control of Noise Pollution

1. A green belt of vegetation (green muffler) could be used. The extra expanse of trees will absorb the noise.

2. Zoning should be specified. In each of these zones, the limit to which noise can be caused is specified.
3. Proper lubricating of machines and equipment will reduce friction and noise.
4. Ear plugs and ear muffs could be used in higher noise areas.
5. Create awareness: no law can do much unless people themselves make an effort. Noise pollution can be curbed by creating awareness and education. When people are aware they will themselves take steps to control pollution.
6. We must conduct research and find better eco-friendly technology that reduces noise pollution.

According to Ministry of Environment and Forests Notification of 14th February, 2000 following are the standards of noise pollution:

Area code	Category of area. Zone	Limits in Db (A)	
		Day time	Night time
A	Industrial area	75	70
B	Commercial area	65	55
C	Residential area	55	45
D	Silence Zone	50	

Solid Waste Pollution

Hotel wastes and their Sources:

- *Garbage*: are both the solid organic and in-organic wastes of varying nature, produced from different sections of in a large hotel:
  - Building: Dusting and sweeping.
  - Gardens: Wood and waste vegetation.
  - Kitchen: Cooked and uncooked food waste.
  - Dining rooms: Left over cooked food waste.
- *Sullage*: comprises of wash water waste from:
  - Bathrooms.
  - Building drains.
  - Kitchen.
- *Sewage*: is the discharge from the water closets.
- *Exhaust gases*: are the gaseous discharge of stale and spent air:
  - Stale air discharge for the general building.
  - Spent air, odor fumes and oil vapor discharge from the kitchen.

- Poisonous gases and spent air from the generator room.
- Chemical waste: From the water treatment plant.

Types of Wastes

Garbage: can be divided in the following components:

- Solid organic waste material:
  - Plastic material scraps.
  - Wooden material scraps.
  - Paper.
  - Linen.
- Solid inorganic materials:
  - Dust from sweeping and dusting.
  - Metal scraps.
  - Glass scraps.
  - Chemicals.
- Liquid organic waste material:
  - Oils.
  - Soap solutions.
  - Sewage drains water.
- Liquid inorganic waste:
  - Sullage drains water.
  - Building-wash drains water.
  - Rainwater.
- Gaseous organic and inorganic waste:
  - Water vapor or moisture.
  - Smoke, which is essentially suspension of carbon particulates in air.
  - Stale air exhaust from the buildings.
  - Fuel waste gases:
    - Form kitchen.
    - Generator exhaust.
  - Oil vapors from kitchen as result of cooking.

General Established Disposal Methods

- *Recycling:* Is the process of material salvages i.e. recovery and reprocessing of waste materials to manufacture of new objects from the processed material. The materials reused in recycling serve as substitutes for the raw materials obtained from increasingly scarce natural resources such as petroleum, natural gas, coal, mineral ores, and trees.

- Recycling can help the following ways:
  - It reduces the quantity of solid waste to be deposited in landfills; land filling has become increasingly difficult due to unavailability vacant land.
  - Recycling reduces the pollution of air, water, and land resulting from the waste disposal.
  - Recycling saves power, which is used to excavate and process the raw materials.
- Typical materials that can be recycled are
  - Solid organic wastes:
    - Paper.
    - Wood.
    - Plastics.
  - Liquid organic waste:
    - Old lubricating oil from engines and machines can be recycled to produce cheap quality lubricating oil for ordinary use.
- Solid inorganic waste:
  - All the metal scraps.
  - All the broken glass scrap.
- Method: after collection from the different sections of the hotel the solid wastes are dumped in different selective bins. The bin materials are then dispatched for the proper recycling process.

❖ *Land filling*: with agreement and permission of the local authorities, the waste materials which have no recycle value are used as filling materials to develop the low lying land areas into level lands; these developed lands can be used to establish new colonies, landscape parks and vegetable or agriculture parks around the city. The landscape parks improve the view of the city and reduce air pollution while vegetable and agriculture parks supplement the food requirement of the local population. The waste material are dumped together with lime and insecticides and covered with layer of earth. As the layer decomposes and settle down new layers are added till the level is a bit higher than the required level. The area is left over for a period to weather and get compacted to settle down to proper level.

- *Disposal in sea*: for the establishment near seashores where waste lowlands are scarce the waste material can be dumped with permission of authorities in the deep sea away from the shores. Care must be taken not to dump such materials into the sea, which may harm the marine and biotic life near the shore. Care is taken to dump the materials in such a way that it does not hamper the sea traffic and that the sea waves may not throw back the waste back on to the shore.
- *Incinerating*: when the dumping facilities are not available or the waste may spread infection, the refuge is burned in incinerators or large-scale refuse burning furnace. The heat developed by burning is used to preheat the new moist waste and also to heat water; the heated water can be used in the establishment for various odd jobs, washing and or heating of building in winter.
- *Irrigation*: the Sullage from the baths and kitchen and building drains is used to irrigate the flora around the hotel site. Care is taken that the water is properly treated and disinfected before use.
- *Cattle feed*: if the hotel maintains its own cattle and poultry farms the cooked and uncooked solid food-waste may be used to feed the animals of the farms; the waste contain good food value and is used to supplement the main animal diet. If the hotel has no such farms of their own the food waste may sold to local farms. With the permission of local authorities it may be dumped in low-lying areas to decompose and turn into manure for use in vegetable farms.
    - The solid wastes form the kitchen, dining rooms etc. is collected at a central isolated place and then machine-compacted into bundles. The bundles are then dispatched for disposal at sites.
- *Disposal in atmosphere*: the general waste gases are vented into the atmosphere. Care is taken to dispose the gases high up in the atmosphere. The discharge from the chimney is kept in the direction of wind flow. Instead of single discharge scattered discharge system is used for better mixing and dilution of the waste gases in the atmosphere.
    - Kitchen exhaust comprising of fuel waste gases and oil vapors needs specialized disposal arrangement and is discussed separately.

Disposal of Kitchen Exhaust Gases: the most common source of energy in the kitchen is hydrocarbon fuels: These fuels on burning produce the following wastes:

- **Ash:** ash becomes a powdered inorganic waste material and causes land pollution.

- ❖ **Gases**: the gaseous due to burning and cooking produce the following components:
  - ❑ **Carbon dioxide**: the average normal level of CO_2 in air is 0.02%. Higher levels cause various levels of discomfort such as headache, dizziness, sleep, and nausea etc.; the gas is mainly responsible for global warming.
  - ❑ **Carbon monoxide**: this gas is produced due to improper and incomplete burning of the fuel. This is a highly poisonous gas; it is responsible for the destruction of the red blood cells of the blood and blood clotting; it thus blocks and reduces the oxygen supply to the tissues causing death.
  - ❑ **Smoke**: Burning of organic fuels is associated with the production of smoke, which contains micron sized carbon ash particles' suspension in waste gases. The micron size suspended particulate matter respiratory problems.
  - ❑ **Cooking fumes**: oil, spices, and other ingredients are used to cook food. The cooking fumes are composed of water and oil vapors and spice smell-chemicals vapors.
  - ❑ **Waste gases** from fuel burning and cooking fumes are responsible for:
    - ✳ Breathing and respiratory problems.
    - ✳ Dirty building interiors and exteriors: on getting cool the water and oil vapors present in the cooking fumes condense on the interior and exterior walls. Dust sticks on the oily surface and make the wall dirty. This process is repetitive and the oil and dust layer thickens with time and it becomes difficult to clean the walls.
    - ✳ Fire hazard: the thick oil-dirt layer may catch fire due to high flue gas temperature. This fire spreads easily and engulfs the combustible materials fixed on the walls.
    - ✳ Food and spice smells cause breathing problem and eye irritation.
- ❖ **Methods of controlling Kitchen Wastes**:
  - ❑ **Control of ash**: The ash content in the solid fuels is highest while lowest in the gaseous fuels. The low ash-content the makes the calorific value of the gaseous fuels highest. Due to these reasons the use of such fuels is very much preferred. The gases commonly used are city gas or L.P.G.

Electric heating is totally ash and smoke less, but due the high cost its use is selective.

- **Control of fly ash**: Fly ash traps must be used in the kitchen exhaust pipe to trap the fly ash. The traps should be cleaned at proper intervals. The collected ash may be use in land filling.
- **Control of carbon mono and dioxide gases**:
  - Use of properly designed burners results in complete combustion and reduces monoxide and un-burnt fuel content.
  - The burners should be so designed as to automatically regulate the air supply for the changing fuel supply, for proper and complete combustion.
- **Control of oil vapors:** The oil vapors of the kitchen fumes should be burnt in pre heaters before they reach the ash traps. The pre-heaters are of two types:
  - Electrically heated.
  - Gas heated.

The heat released from the burning of the oil vapors is used to heat water, which can be used for dish and utensil washing.

Disposal of sewage: If facilities are available the sewage from the toilets is dumped in the local municipal sewer system. In case such facility is not available the hotel will have to establish and maintain its own sewage treatment plant.

SEWAGE TREATMENT PLANT

The sewage is treated properly and disinfected according to the local rules. The clean water from the treatment plant is used to irrigate lawns and flora of the hotel. The treated sewage slurry is dried in open land in sun to turn into goods quality manure cakes; this may be either used in the hotel gardens or sold.

Water is treated in waste water treatment plants or effluent treatment plants. Such treatment plants treat water in three phases:

Primary treatment: this involves removal of large solids. It is mostly done by using screens and filters. These remove the large solids from waste water.

Secondary treatment: this is the second step of treatment. In secondary treatment the biological degradation of organic wastes in waste water is done by micro-organisms.

Tertiary treatment: this involves the removal of wastes that could be removed by primary and secondary treatment. Many methods are employed depending on nature of waste. Some methods used are reverse osmosis, activated carbon etc.

Septic Tank

A sewage treatment process commonly used to treat domestic wastes is the septic tank: a concrete, cinder block or metal tank where the solids settle and the floatable materials rise. The partly clarified liquid stream flows from a submerged outlet into subsurface rock-filled trenches through which the wastewater can flow and percolate into the soil where it is oxidized aerobically. The floating matter and settled solids can be held from six months to several years, during which they are decomposed anaerobically.

Generator exhaust: it is essential for big hotels to maintain their own emergency backup electric power arrangement. Diesel generator sets are generally used for his purpose. The exhaust from the gen.-sets is very irritating and contains carbon particulates, carbon mono/dioxide and cancer producing gases. At the same time the sets produce lot of vibration and noise. To contain these conditions the following methods are used:

- The gen-sets should be installed in proper rooms at a distance from the main hotel building to reduce vibration and noise.
- Vibration absorbing pads, and noise suppressing arrangement are provided.
- The gen-set room should be so oriented so that the exhaust is driven away from the main building with the natural airflow moist of the time of the year.
- The exhaust is disposed through high chimneys with traps for the solid particulates.
- Multi discharge system is used to dilute the waste gases.

Chemical wastes: If the hotel is not getting the municipal water it has to manage its own water supply through deep tube-wells. The water from these well may require chemical and disinfecting treatment to make it potable. The chemical waste from the treatment plants should be discharged for dilution in water mass or drying up in pits, according to the local health and safety regulations.

SUMMARY

If we compare hotel industry of 1930 with the industry of today's. We find that more and more appliances, techniques are being in most modern hotels and catering units. These appliance and techniques are being used to make a comfortable, safe and secure stay of the resident guests. Some of these appliances are used in kitchen such as micro wave ovens, deep freezers, blast refrigerators etc and others are used by different departments of the hotels including hotel engineering, front office, house keeping, food and beverage service etc. all these appliances are contributing either in a small or big manner a type of pollution ranging from air to noise. Guests are using automobiles to check in or checkout and contributing a lot of vehicular pollution. Being an eco friendly manager it become our responsibility to reduce pollution by using various new technologies and creating awareness to our fellow colleagues and by following norms of pollution control boards and other Acts.

Modern hotel industry has developed very dangerous trends. We have developed an insatiable desire for more and more new products. Everyday we have newer products and techniques being launched. Our consumption has multiplied many folds because we want more and more. All of this has an effect on natural resources. Due to overexploitation most of our resources have dwindled and that is the reason we have shortage of clean air, clean water and overall clean environment which is a basic need of a common human being including our guests.

CONCEPT REVIEW QUESTIONS

1. Enlist types of pollution in reference to hotel and catering industry.
   - ❖ Pollutants
   - ❖ Solid waste
   - ❖ Incineration
   - ❖ Pesticides
   - ❖ Sanitary landfills
   - ❖ Recycling
   - ❖ Sewage
   - ❖ Greenhouse effect
   - ❖ Pollution control equipment
   - ❖ Ozone layer depletion
2. Being an owner of a catering unit how you will control noise pollution.
3. Explain impacts of air pollution on human life.
4. Enlist techniques of controlling solid waste pollution adopted by hotels.
5. Explain working of a sewage treatment plant.
6. How research work on improved technology can help in reducing pollution in hotel and catering industry.
7. Name a law that is aimed at controlling air pollution.
8. Name any two water borne diseases.
9. Mentioned two ways by which hotel industry harm the environment and suggest controlling measures too.

10. Setting emission standards are good way of controlling noise pollution. Justify

Project Assignments

1. Discuss with chief engineer of a hotel about their installed pollution controlling measures and techniques.
2. Check relevance of creating awareness about pollution in nearby hotel of your town, prepare a report and discuss in your classroom.
3. Zoning is a better way to control noise pollution. Examine various destinations of your city with their noise level.
4. Take a glass slide and smear it with Vaseline. Suspend it in a crowded place where there is a lot of air pollution. Many of the pollutants will get stuck to it. This will give you a rough estimate of the amount of pollution in an area. Compare pollution levels in different areas using this method.

9

EQUIPMENT REPLACEMENT POLICIES

LEARNING OBJECTIVES

By the end of the lesson you will be able to:

- Explain circumstances under which equipment are replacement in hotel and catering industry
- Explain policies of equipment replacement
- Calculate time for equipment replacement

INTRODUCTION

Equipment, plant and machinery are very important for achieving guest satisfaction. Substantial part of the investment in hotel industry is in its physical plant. It is more economical to replace equipment before it completely breaks down.

There are two types of equipments:

1. Which gradually deteriorates for example: air conditioning plant, washing machine?
2. Suddenly fails for example: bulbs, electrical circuit breakers.

Equipment which gradually deteriorates is replaced in the following circumstances:

- **Inadequacy** means existing one may be incapable of meeting the increasing demand. So an alternative which can meet demand will be installed.
- **Obsolescence** refers to a new equipment is continually being develop that will perform the same operations as the existing one, but substantial savings can be gained by replacement.
- **Excessive maintenance** means that machines and other complex equipments rarely incurred uniform wear. Some elements or components are likely to deteriorate faster and failed before others.

- ❖ **Declining efficiency** stands for equipment sometimes operates at an initial peak efficiency which declines with time and use. The reduction efficiency may require increase power consumption and more time.
- ❖ **Replacement due to combination of causes.**

Maximizing utilization resources employed is fundamental to attaining the profit goals of any business. Capital or finance has to be managed efficiently under changing environment; be it the investment on fixed assets, or the working capital. The need for replacement arises from the inevitable fact but no item in service can last indefinitely. By replacement of spare parts repeatedly and taking up repairs continually, it may be theoretically possible to prolong a life of a machine indefinitely, but this can not be economical policy. The problem is to determine the times at which such remedial actions should be taken.

DETERMINATION OF REPLACEMENT CYCLE FOR EQUIPMETS, WHICH FAIL SUDDENLY WITHOUT ANY INDICATION OR DO NOT HAVE A PROBABLE DEFINITE LIFE TIME

1. The only truth for suddenly failing equipments is that they will fail someday without any indication whatsoever.
2. The average life in such cases can be ascertained by probability concept.
3. Probability is defined as the ratio of 'number of favorable cases of occurrences' to the 'total number of possible cases'.
4. Classic example is that of the incandescent lamps, a lamp will either be healthy or fused; hence the probability of its being healthy is one in two conditions, hence the probability of its being healthy is only 50%. With an average life of 1000 working hours for lamp of certain wattage means the probability of a particular lamp to operate for 1000 hours is only 50%. Another way to express it is, if 1000 lamps are installed at one time, and all are operated under identical conditions for equal length of time, only 500 would be in operation after 1000 hours of use. Therefore average life of equipment is the period when one half or 50% of the Equipment Population will fail.

   Figure shows a mortality curve for such items
5. A manufacturer's warranty is normally based on such an average life curve. Warranty period increases as the average life of the product increases.
6. Under such circumstances the cost of immediate individual replacement i.e. Spot replacement at times is much more higher than the actual cost of the equipment itself.

7. A typical example is that of electric lamps whose failing is uncertain. If a lamp costs Rs.10.00 and the labor cost of 'spot' (immediate individual) replacement\ of a failing lamp is about Rs.20.00. The total cost of spot replacing a lamp sums up to Rs.30.00. Also every time a lamp is changed there is an associated loss due to customers discomfort and dissatisfaction.
8. The replacement cost involves the item cost together with the labor cost, therefore the total batch of the equipment should replaced at such a frequency when the average total cost comprising that of the equipment together with the labor replacement cost is minimum.

Considerations

1. The replacement cycle for suddenly failing equipment is known as 'Group Replacement'.
2. If the manufacturer's data are not available then the users will have to experiment themselves to determine the group replacement frequency.
3. In such case of indefinite failure it is assumed that the efficiency of the equipment is stable over its lifetime. The group replacement procedure is economically feasible when the cost of labor is very high compared to the cost of the equipment replaced.
4. The cost of labor includes the man-hours for the preparation, actual removal, installation and cleanup jobs. If done on routine basis for every individual lamp failure it will prove to be a very costly affair and at the same time it will be a cause of discomfort and irritation to the guests.
5. It will be a better and cheaper proposition to change all the lamps in one operation at a proper time when the total cost is minimum.
6. An initial cycle of replacement is to be assumed for analysis. The procedure will provide and ideal cycle of replacement. The replacement cycle time can be expressed in days, weeks, months or even years.

   The failure data should be reasonable to assess the operating life of the equipment. Once the information is obtained regarding the proposed cycle of replacement and the rate of failure the remaining data is based on the cost of labor and material for the replacement.
7. The cost of individual replacement is compared to the cost per unit for group replacement.
8. The cost of item is also considered. If large number of the item is purchased at one time, the quantity purchase discount is available, which may lower cost for group replacement.

9. In the group replacement all the items are changed at one time and a majority of these items are discarded or sold as scrap. Some are retained for future spot replacement.

Case Study 1

Initial cost of a laundry machine is Rs. 70,000. its value if sold is Rs. 50,000 after one year, Rs. 40,000 after two year, Rs. 30,000 after three year .it loses 20% of the remaining value in each subsequent year. Its operating cost includes maintenance, cost of spares and loss of output is Rs. 2,000 in first year, Rs.4,000 in two year and so on, increasing by Rs.2,000 a year each. When the machine is due for replacement.

Case Study 2

An electronic company has a highly specialized precision machine with also a high rate of obsolescence. In spite of regular maintenance, the quality of output of the machine deteriorates fast and adversely affects the percent acceptable components and the revenue. It is required to determine the time when machines of this type would be due for replacement. The following data are available from past records.

Year	1	2	3	4	5
Yearly gross earning from sales	22,000	17,000	10,000	6,000	3,500
Yearly expenses	1,500	2,000	2,500	3,000	3,002
Salvage value at the end of the year	**10,000.00**	**8,000.00**	**5,000.00**	**1,000.00**	**500.00**

If the installed cost of the machine is Rs. 25,000 and expected rate of return for company investments is 10%. Find the economic life of the machine.

Solutions

End of year	1	2	3	4	5
Net earning from sales	20,500	15,000	7,500	3,000	498
Discount factor (1 + I) t	.909	.826	.751	.683	.621
Present value of net earning = 2 3	18634.50	12390.00	5632.50	2049.00	309.25

Solutions

Year	Value at end of year 70,000	Depreciation in the year	Operating cost	Total cost in the year	Cumulative total cost	Average cost / year
1.	50,000	20,000.00	2,000	22,000.00	22,000.00	22000.00
2.	40,000	10,000.00	4,000	14,000.00	36,000.00	18,000.00
3.	30,000	10,000.00	6,000	16,000.00	52,000.00	17333.33
4.	24,000	6,000.00	8,000	14000.00	66000.00	16500.00
5.	19,200	4,800.00	10,000	14,800.00	80800.00	16160.00
6.	15,360	3840.00	12,000	15840.00	96640.00	**16106.66**
7.	12,288	3072.00	14,000	17072.00	113712.00	16244.57
8.	9830.40	2457.60	16,000	18457.60	132169.60	16521.20
9.	7864.32	1960.08	18,000	19960.08	152129.68	16903.29

Thus the minimum average annual cost is Rs.16106.00 and is obtained by replacing machine every 6 years. So machine is due for replacement after six years.

Present value of salvage	9090.00	6608.00	3755.00	683.00	310.50
Cumulative present value	27724.50	37632.50	40412.00	39389.00	39325.75
Net present value = 6 – 25,000	2724.50	12632.50	15412.00	14389.00	14325.75

The net present value starts decreasing from 4th year so it is advisable to replace the machine after every three year.

Concept of Probability

The average life of equipment can be determined by the help pf probability concept. The probability is the ratio between favorable cases to the total number of possible cases.

Replacement Cycles for Items that Fail (group replacement)

The only certain fact regarding equipment is that someday it will fail. The exact time can only be estimated from probability theory. The classic example in the bulb that has an average life of 1000 hours for certain wattage normal life lamps. All this means is that the probability of a particular lamp operating 1000 hours is 50%. If 1000 lamps were installed at one time, and if all were operated for an equal length of time, only 500 would still bc in opcration aftcr 1000 hours of usc. Most failure curves follow the same general shape. A manufacturer's warranty is based on such curves. Warranty periods increase as the estimated life of the product increases. If manufacturer data are not available and large numbers of units are installed in a building these mortality curves can be developed for a particular operation.

The replacement of items that fail generally assumes that the efficiency of the unit is stable over its life. If the efficiency does not significantly vary from its initial value to its failure, the procedure that follows can be used to analyze and develop replacement cycles.

This procedure becomes economically feasible when the cost of labor is very high in relation to the cost of the item being replaced. The costs of labor include the preparation, removal, installation and clean up man-hours for replacing items. It also assumes that if items fail prematurely, they will be replaced on a route basis. Hence sending an electrician to a guest room to replace a burned-out lamp can become very costly. The electrician may start from the location of the engineering and maintenance department, walk to the room, remove and install a new electric lamp, and return to his department. If all of this time is accumulated, the cost of changing one lamp could be very expensive. It may be better to replace all the lamps in the room while the electrician is there. These at least will greatly lower the average cost per lamp.

An initial cycle of replacement must be assumed for the analysis. The procedure will provide an ideal cycle of replacement.

The cycle of replacement may be expressed in hours, days, months or years. The estimates must be reasonable if an operating life is assumed. Once information is obtained regarding the proposed cycle of replacement and the rate of failure, the remaining data is based on the cost labor and material for replacement. The cost of individual or spot replacement is compared to the cost per unit for group replacement. Generally these are estimated average costs. But if previous data are available for a particular property that should be used.

The cost of an item is also considered. If large numbers of items are purchased at one time, quantity discounts may be available which may lower unit costs for group replacement. In a group replacement all items are removed at one time and the majority of these items are discarded. Some are retained for future spot replacement.

Case Study 3

The following mortality rates have been observed for a certain type of light bulb:

Week	1	2	3	4	5
% failing by end of week	10	25	50	80	100

There are 1000 bulbs in use and it costs Rs. 3 to replace an individual bulb which has burnt out. If all bulbs are replaced simultaneously it would cost Rs. 1 per bulb. If is proposed to replace all bulbs at fixed intervals, whether or not they have burnt out and to continue replacing burnt out bulbs as they fail.

At what intervals should all the bulbs be replaced.

Solution

We first compute the probability that a new bulb fails in successive week (no group replacement in operation). Let P1 denote the probability that a bulb which was new then installed fails during the ith week of its life. The probability is clearly the difference between the proportion alive at the end of ith week and the proportion alive at the end of the ith week. We obtain the probability as follows:

Week	1	2	3	4	5	Total
Probability that a new bulb installed at time zero fails during week I (p)	.10	.15	.25	.30	.20	1.0

Note: That no installed bulb survives more than 5 weeks. Thus a bulb that has already lasted 4 weeks is sure to fail the fifth week. However, the unconditional probability of failure during the fifth week for a new bulb installed at time zero is what we are denoting by ps and has the value 0.20.

With two simplifying assumptions, we can compute the number of replacement due to failure in successive weeks under a policy of no group replacement. We assume:

1. That bulb fails during a week are replaced just before the end of the week.
2. That the actual % of failures during a week for a subpopulation of bulbs with the same age is the same as expected % of failures during the week for the subpopulation.

Let n1 denote the number of replacements made at the end of the ith week of all 1000 bulbs are new initially. Then under our assumption we immediately obtain.

n 0 = n = 1000

n 1 = n 0p1 = 100

n 2 = n 0p2 + n 1p1 =150 + 10 = 160

n 3 = n 0 p3+ n 1p2 + n 2 p1 = 281

n 4 = n 0p4 + n 1 p3 + n2 p2 + n 3 p1 = 377

n 5 = n0 p5 + n1p4 + n2p3 + n3p2+ n4p1 = 350

It will be noticed that the number of bulbs failing each week increases until week 4 and then decreases. It can be shown that the number will later start to increase and it will continue to oscillate until ultimate systems settle down to a steady state in which proportion of bulbs failing each week I the reciprocal of their average life. The average life is (1x.10)+ (2x.15)+ (3x.25)+(4x.20) + (5x.20) = 3.35 weeks. In the steady state, the number of failures each week will be 1000/ 3.35 =299 bulbs. Hence the failure replacement policy will cost 299 x 3 = Rs.897.00 per week.

Let us compare and find the optimum replacement cycle.

Thus it would be cheapest to replace all the bulbs every three weeks.

Case Study 4: Life Cycle Costing

A hotel had an air-conditioning system that could continue to operate for another ten years. Its present estimated value is Rs. 50,000. Maintenance cost including cost of spares has been closed to Rs. 5,000 per year. Energy cost on the unit is Rs. 15000 per year. Its anticipated salvage value in 10 years is Rs. 10,000.

The chief engineer has an estimate for a new air conditioner that will consume only Rs.7,000 on energy in the next year. The installation cost of the equipment is Rs. 80,000. its average repair and maintenance expenses will probably be Rs. 4,000 per year over the next ten years. It will have a salvage value of Rs. 10,000 in 10 years.

Energy costs are expected to increase at 10 % per year for the next 10 years. The current hotel interest rate (cost of borrowing money) is 14%. Should the chief engineer recommend the new air conditioner or keep the current unit.

Solution

The basic relationship that can be used to determine the present value of estimated cost is shown below:

Total present cost = present cost of equipment + future maintenance and repair costs + future energy costs – salvage value

$$TC = A + B\,F1 + CF2F3 - SF3$$

Where

TC = total present value costs

A = initial cost including installation

B = estimated annual repair and maintenance costs

F1 = factor that when applied to annual costs will equate these to present value

C = estimated annual energy costs

F2 = factor that adjusts for the rising cost of energy; if energy costs are not expected to increase the value of F2 is 1.

F3 = factor that when applied to (CF2) or S will equate these to present value

S = salvage value

Alternative 1: keep present unit

A = Rs. 50,000

B = Rs. 5,000

Optimum replacement cycle

Week	Probability	Total nos. of failed	Cumulative no. of failure	Cost of replacement after failure	Cost of previous. replacement	Total cost	Average cost/ week
1	.10	100	100	300	1000	1300	1300
2	.15	160	260	780	1000	1780	890
3	.25	281	541	1623	1000	2623	874
4	.30	377	918	2754	1000	3754	938
5	.20	350	1268	3804	1000	4804	961

C = Rs. 15,000

F1 = 5.22 for 10 years (N) and 14% (I)

F2 = 15.9 for 10 years (N) and 10% (I)

F3 = 0.270 for 10 years (N) and 14% (I)

S = Rs. 10,000

TC1 = 50,000 + 5,000 (5.22) + 15,000 (15.9) (0.270) – 10,000 (0.270)

= 50,000 + 26,100 + 64395 – 2700

= 1,37,795.00

If this amount of money is placed in an account earning 14% interest. It would cover all present and future costs.

Alternative 2: purchase a new air conditioner.

A = Rs. 80,000

B = Rs. 4,000

C = Rs. 7,000

F1 = 5.22 for 10 years (N) and 14% (I)

F2 = 15.9 for 10 years (N) and 10% (I)

F3 = 0.270 for 10 years (N) and 14% (I)

S = Rs. 10,000

TC2 = 80,000 + 5,000 (5.22) + 7,000 (15.9) (0.270) – 10,000 (0.270)

= 80,000 + 26,100 + 30,051 – 2770

= 1,36,151.00

If this amount of money is placed in an account earning 14% interest. It would cover all present and future costs.

Difference = 1,37,795 – 1,36,151 = Rs. 1644

Comparison

The difference of Rs. 1644.00 is very small – the chief engineer would probably recommend that the present unit be retained. Actually both units are almost cost effective, if energy costs were to increase at a higher rate than 10% in future; alternative 2 will be more attractive.

SUMMARY

This chapter has considered questions the engineer/hospitality manager should address when equipment is due for replacement keeping in view the economic life.

As it must be discretion of a technical staff to look into the matter technically but above mentioned case studies may help a technician to look into the matter in terms of economic life of the equipment as millions of rupees has been invested by the owner of hotel and catering property.

CONCEPT REVIEW QUESTIONS

1. Enlist causes of equipment replacement.
2. Describe following terms:
   - ❑ Inadequacy
   - ❑ Obsolescence
   - ❑ Excessive maintenance.
   - ❑ Declining efficiency
3. Being an owner of a catering unit how you will decide when an equipment is due for replacement.

Numerical Problems

1. Initial cost of a deep freezer is Rs. 80,000. its value if sold is Rs. 55,000 after one year, Rs. 45,000 after two year, Rs. 35,000 after three year .it loses 15% of the remaining value in each subsequent year. Its operating cost includes maintenance, cost of spares and loss of output is Rs. 3,000 in first year, Rs.5,000 in two year and so on, increasing by Rs.2,500 a year each. When deep freezer is due for replacement.
2. An IT company has a highly specialized precision machine with also a high rate of obsolescence. In spite of regular maintenance, the quality of output of the machine deteriorates fast and adversely affects the percent acceptable components and the revenue. It is required to determine the time when machines of this type would be due for replacement. The following data are available from past records.

Year	1	2	3	4	5
Yearly gross earning from sales	35,000	30,000	250,000	16,000	13,500
Yearly expenses	4,500	5,000	5,500	6,000	6,200
Salvage value at the end of the year	**10,000.00**	**8,000.00**	**5,000.00**	**1,000.00**	**500.00**

If the installed cost of the machine is Rs. 45,000 and expected rate of return for company investments is 10%. Find the economic life of the machine.

PROJECT ASSIGNMENTS

Discuss with a chief engineer of a hotel about their strategies adopted for equipment replacement especially for heavy duty equipment and compare with strategies adopted for light equipment and find why they are differ.

10

WATER SUPPLY SYSTEM

LEARNING OBJECTIVES

By the end of the lesson you will be able to:

- Explain types of taps, traps, flushing cistern and closets used in hotel and catering industry
- Define water hardness and explain its causes
- Explain water softening techniques
- Explain types of water distribution system used in hotel and catering industry
- Explain types of water distribution system used in hotel and catering industry

INTRODUCTION

There are three most important distribution systems in the hospitality industry operate on primary energy sources: Fuel for heating, electric power and water. Water is most important amongst all and generally water provides by a public utility similar to electrical energy. Hospitality industries are totally dependent on supply of potable water and sanitary drainage network system. Proper supply of clean water is becoming a global issue now a days and every country is putting their efforts to ensure supply of safe, hygienic and clean water to their citizens. Water has become a very important energy resource. As we are aware that primary source of fresh water are lakes, rivers and ground water and because of pollution, rivers and lakes are polluted so there is an only one source remains that is underground. Extraction of water from the ground also becoming a serious problem because label of water in most of the areas are falling down, so there is an immediate need of recycling of water and its conservation. Water must be treated to make it potable, that is, safe for human consumption. Treatment process depends on amount of water to be treated and on quality of extracted water.

PLUMBING ACCESSORIES AND SANITORY FITTINGS

The following and accessories are commonly used in Plumbing and Sanitation work. The fittings are made either of cast iron, galvanized cast iron or galvanized iron. Surface of iron is galvanized with zinc to resist corrosion and to improve appearance. Certain fittings such as taps and showers etc. used in bathrooms, water closets, washbasins and kitchen are fabricated of brass are electroplated with nickel, chromium, silver or gold to improve appearance and cleanness.

The commonly used pipefittings are listed below:

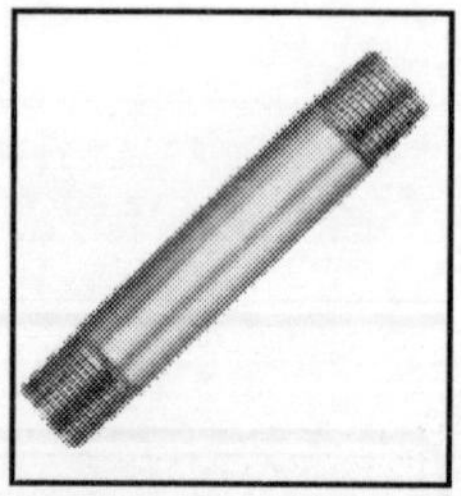

- *Galvanized iron pipe*: it is made of galvanized steel and in used to convey water from source to the point of use. They are available in standard length and different sections to meet the water delivery rate. The commonly used bore sections are 12, 18, 25, 31, 38 and 50 mm. However higher bore sections such as 75, 100 and 150 mm are also available. The pipes are available with outer treads at both ends for joining and extension facility.
- *G.I. Socket or Bushing*: they are small pieces of G.I. pipes with internal threads at both the ends to suit the outer threads of the pipes. For extension the pipes are screwed on both the ends of the socket. The pipes joints are made with cord and binding paste on the screw threads while fixing to check leakage. The sockets are available in sizes to suit the pipe dimension e.g. 12,18, 25, 31, 38 mm and so on.
- *G.I. Reducing socket*: we require a reducing socket when a particular section pipe is to be joined with a different section pipe. The two ends of the socket are suitably sized and threaded to accommodate the two different sections of pipes. For example reducing socket of 25x12mm socket is used to connect pipes of 25 and 12mm pipes.
- *G.I. bend*: bends are used for smooth change of the direction of the pipes. Commonly used bends are 90° angle.
- *G.I. Elbow*: are modified sockets with a sharp bend at the middle. Elbow is used when the pipe is extension requires sharp change in direction. The commonly used elbows are of 45 and 90^0 angle.
- *G.I. Tee*: tee is a modified socket with an extension socket at 90^0 in the middle. It is used when we have to tap an extension branch, off the main running pipe at right angle.
- *Reducing Tee*: is required when a smaller section extension pipe is required to branch off a larger section pipe.
- *G.I. Cross*: is a modified Tee when two extension pipes in opposite directions are to be branched off at the same point of the main pipe. Crosses are available to accommodate large section main pipe and small sections of branch pipes.

- *G.I. Union*: unions are essential for facility of fitting and dismantling pipes at single or double bends zones of the pipe run. A cheaper alternative to union is running socket arrangement.
- *G.I.Cap*: cap is an internally threaded socket with one end closed or blocked. They are screwed on the open end of a pipe threads to check water wastage.
- *G.I. Plug*: are externally threaded solid blocks with a square-tightening end. They are screwed in the open socket ends of pipe to check water wastage when replacing taps etc.
- Gate valves are used as on- off valves. They are operated either in completely closed or opened positions. Their resistance to water flow is minimal. These are used as shut-off valves on water mains.

Gate valves

- Angle and globe valves are used for variable water flow. They have a high resistance to water flow when partially opened; thus, they restrict water flow. When completely opened, they have moderate resistance. These are used in bathtubs, showers, sinks and lavatories.
- Check valves allow water to flow only one way, have minimal resistance, and act as shut-off valves for reversed water flow.
- Fast- acting gate valves are key valves, which normally require only a 90-to 180 degree (quarter to half –turn on handle to be fully opened or closed).

Angle and Globe Valves

Commonly Used Sanitary Fittings

- *Taps*: taps are fittings, which control (open or close) and regulate (vary) water supply. The commonly used taps are listed below:

Bib cock/Tap: this tap is fixed at the end of horizontal extension of the main pipe. These taps are provided with screwed handles and washers to control and regulate water flow. Cheaper versions of taps are simply brass taps while the decorative and costlier versions are chromium or even gold plated.

BIB TAP

Taps are devices, which control (check or allow) and regulate the flow of water. Bib tap are the taps, which are fixed at the end of the horizontal extension of pipe.

Parts of Bib Tap

- *Screwed rod*: it is a short length or gunmetal rod. This rod is provided external threads on lower end and a cross bar, riveted or screw fixed at the top end. There is a small short length hole at the bottom end to keep the washer holder centrally in place.
- *Screwed nut*: a screwed nut is tightened on the valve body. The screwed nut is provided with internal threads at the lower end in which the screwed rod operates. At the top end of the screwed nut there is a 'Gland box', which is internally threaded. This gland box is stuffed with packing and compressed tight by the gland nut.
- *Gland packing*: gland packing is made of lubricated asbestos rope length. The packing is coiled on the screwed rod and packed tight in the gland box and then compressed with the gland nut. The compressed gland packing prevents water leakage by the sides of the screwed rod.
- *Washer holder and washer*: the shape of the washer holder is show in the figure. It consists of a circular plate with short small diameter extensions on both ends. The top extension is plain and is held in the bottom hole of the screwed rod, while the bottom extension is screwed. A centrally holed leather or nylon washer is fixed on the bottom extension with the help of a nut.
- *Tap body*: The specially designed tap body is made of brass or gunmetal. On the topside there is internally threaded hole to receive the screwed nut. At one side there is externally threaded inlet extension, which tightens on the pipe. On the other side there is downward directed water out let. In between the two sides there is a specially designed horizontal partition. The top face of the hole is machined so that the washer sits flush on it without leakage when tightened with the screwed rod.
- *Working*:
  - When the cross bar is rotated clockwise it drives the screwed rod downwards.
  - This pushes the washer holder at the bottom.
  - The washer is pressed tight on the partition hole.
  - This checks the water flow.
  - When the cross bar is rotated counter clockwise the screwed bar moves up.
  - The washer becomes loose on the partition hole.
  - The pressure of the water lifts the washer holder and starts flowing.

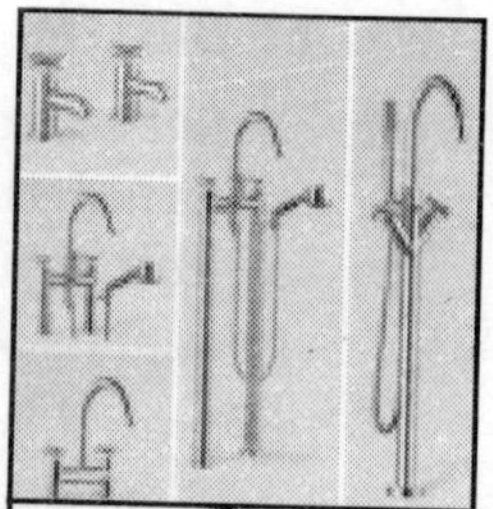

Pillar tap: this tap is designed to fit at the end of a vertical pipe. The common use of this tap is in washbasins and bathtubs. The control arrangement and the types are similar to the bib tap.

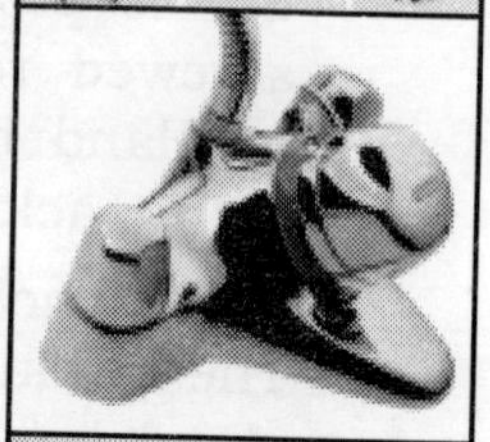

Gravity Tap: this tap is self-closing. Instead of screw control a waterspout weight is attached to the washer holder. Pushing the weight up allows water to flow while on releasing the weight it drops under gravity and pulls the washer down with it. This automatically checks the water flow. This tap is useful in public areas and with water coolers to check water wastage out of negligence.

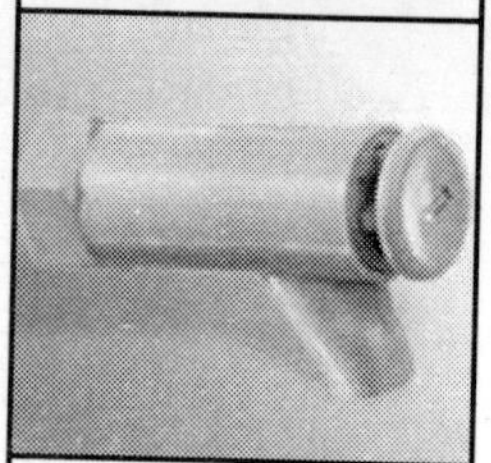

Push cock: this is a variation of self-closing tap in which the closing action is spring actuated. On pressing the control knob the valve opens and at the same time a spring under the knob is compressed. On removing pressure on the knob the spring releases and closes the valve.

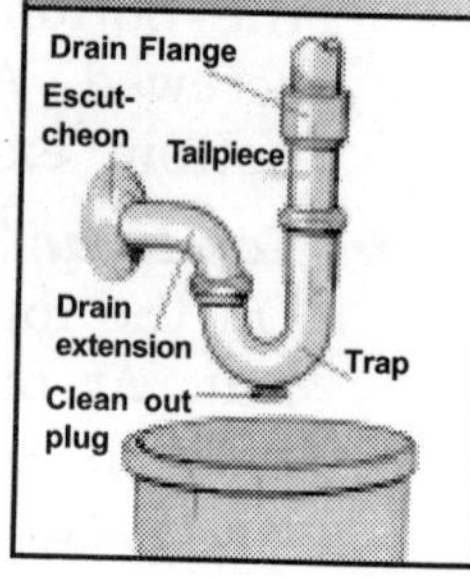

Traps: traps are essentially fitted on the receiving end of water waste outlet pipes of kitchen, washbasin, bathroom floors and water closets. It consists of water receiving cup with a sieve cover. At the bottom the cup is connected to a short, horizontal U-shaped pipe. The upper end of the cup with the sieve is fixed slightly below the floor surface. The sieve checks the entry of debris in the trap and choking of the trap and pipe. The opening of the U-shaped extension of the trap is connected to the out-let pipe, which conveys the sullage out of the building. After the water is drained out of the building a little amount of water remains trapped in the U-shaped pipe. This trapped water forms a water-seal, and prevents the entry of insects and foul gases from out side to the interior of the building.

WATER CISTERNS

Water cisterns are used to flush water closets. They work on the principle of 'Siphon'. They are generally of three types:

- ❖ Bell type water cistern.
- ❖ Plunger type water cistern.
- ❖ Automatic water cistern.

1. Bell type water cistern:

- ❖ Parts:
  - ❑ Cistern tank and Cover: Made of cast iron and work for storing water in covered cistern.

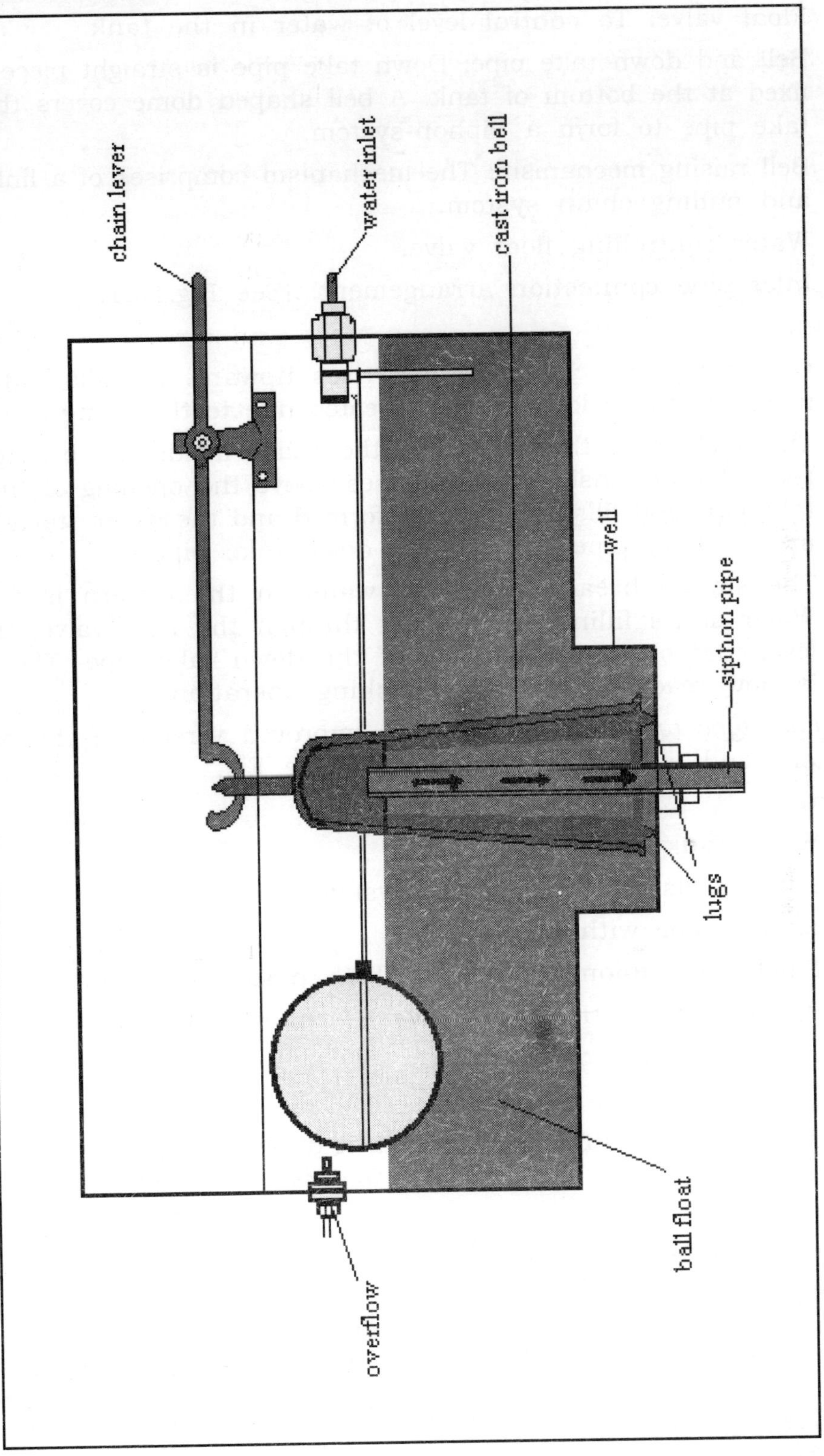
chain lever
water inlet
cast iron bell
well
siphon pipe
lugs
ball float
overflow

Fig.10.1

- ❑ Float valve: To control level of water in the tank.
- ❑ Bell and down take pipe: Down take pipe is straight piece of pipe fixed at the bottom of tank. A bell shaped dome covers the down take pipe to form a Siphon-system.
- ❑ Bell raising mechanism: The mechanism comprises of a link, lever, and pulling chain system.
- o Water controlling float valve.
- o Inlet pipe connection arrangement. (See Fig.10.1)

❖ Working:

- ❑ On pulling the chain the bell rises upward. It pulls water level inside it due to low pressure created due to the rising of the bell.
- ❑ The sucking of the water fills the space inside the bell top. The level of water inside the bell rises above the opening of the down take pipe and fills it. Siphon is formed and the water starts flowing in the flush pipe through the down take pipe.
- ❑ The siphon breaks when the water in the cistern is finished. Water starts filling in the tank through the float valve, up to a level just below the opening of the down take pipe. The cistern is now ready for the next flushing operation.

2. *Plunger type water cistern*: It is an improved version of the bill type cistern and is now generally used. (See Fig. 10.1)

❖ Parts:

- ❑ Water tank and cover.
- ❑ Plunger piston and cylinder system.
- ❑ Siphon pipe with inlet valve.
- ❑ Flush pipe union and plastic flush pipe.
- ❑ Water level control float valve.
- ❑ Inlet pipe connection union.

❖ Working:

- ❑ When the operating rod is pulled, it draws the plunger piston with it in the plunger cylinder; due to this water is drawn up in the cylinder.
- ❑ Water pressure closes the water inlet valve and the water is pushed in the siphon pipe.
- ❑ The siphon action is actuated and the water starts flowing in the down take pipe. Due to suction action the inlet valve gets open and the tank water enters the siphon and continues to flow. The flushing action goes on till the water level in the tank falls below

the inlet valve when air is sucked in and the siphon action breaks. The piston drops down due to its weight.

- Water inlet float valve opens and the tank is filled for the next operation.

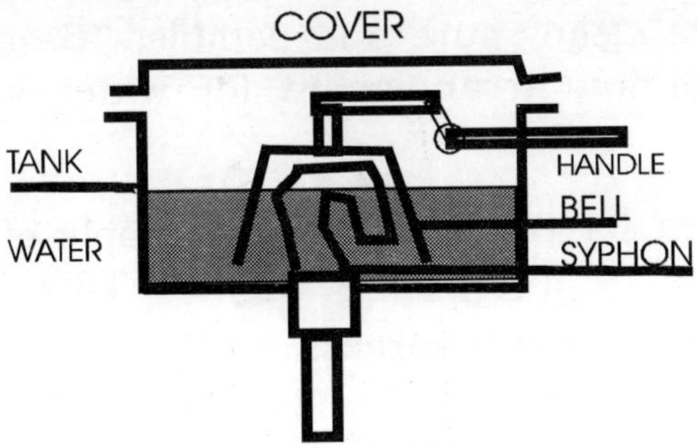

Fig. 10.2

3. *Automatic operating cisterns*: only siphon pipe is fitted in the tank. Water enters directly at a very slow rate and when the level of the water fills up the siphon, the cistern flushes till it is empty. As the water is continuing filling slowly the flushing repeats after some time automatically. Such cisterns are fitted in public place urinals or water closets, which are in continuous use.

Sources of Water

Chemically, water is hydrogen oxide (H_2O). It is available on earth in all the three phases of matter. It participates in practically every ecosystem process and is vital for the living world.

Total earth water available covers about 71% of the earth's surface. The total quantity of water on earth is estimated at about 1400-mega cubic kilometer or 1.400_x10^9 cubic km. Expressed in liters 1.4_x10^{18} cubic meter or 1.4_x10^{21} liter or 1.4_x10^{21} kg approximately. The main approximate distributions of the water on earth is mentioned below:

- Oceans: 97.0%
- Ice caps and Glaciers: 2.2%
- Under-Ground reservoirs: 0.6%
- Lakes, rivers, Soil moisture Biosphere, Atmosphere: 0.2%

Total 100.0 %

Drinking Water Sources

The drinking water sources can be divided mainly as:

- *Ground Water sources*: rivers and big lakes constitute the main ground water sources. This being the reason those big ancient civilizations settled near riverbanks and perennial lakes.

- *Under ground water sources*: Ancient people had the knowledge about the under ground water. They tapped it by digging shallow wells. With advancement of time and technology new and better types of wells were designed which could pump out large quantities of water from deep underground water reservoirs. The water from deep underground is plentiful, more clean, pure and potable. These days deep bore tube wells are a common arrangement for water supply.

Water Supply System

It is the arrangement for transporting and supply of water from the areas of abundance to areas of need or deficiency. This includes:

- Tapping the land water sources:
  - Installations are constructed for the collection of raw water at the land water sources such as rivers and lakes and subsequent treatment to make it potable. The collection and treatment plants collectively are called 'Water works'. Main sections of water works are:
    - Pumping stations: high capacity pumps installed by the side of raw water sources deliver large quantities of water. These pumps are generally located near the river entry end of the city in order to get comparatively clean and less polluted raw water.
    - Installations for treatment of water: the raw water from the pumping station is transported through pipes to large filtration tanks, which remove suspended impurities. The clean water is treated with coagulating agents to settle finer suspended impurities and then with chemicals to disinfect it. After this it is aerated to remove bad odors and to dissolve oxygen and carbon dioxide, all this makes the water potable and tasty.
    - Transportation and distribution network: the potable water is then transported to distribution centers and then to homes, commercial establishments, industry, public utility establishments and services, and irrigation through a distribution pipe network.
- Underground water sources: in the present days of high technology deep underground water sources are generally tapped on a large scale to supply water for population settlements away from rivers and also to supplement supply to big riverside cities. The waters from deep tube wells require less treatment as it is comparatively clean and free from bacteria. Sometimes the water contains harmful dissolved chemicals, for which the water is suitably treated before supply.

- ❑ Numbers of tube wells are bored at suitable places in the settlement with large capacity overhead storage tanks for emergency. The pumping stations are interconnected in a net work for better supply pressure and to maintain continuity of water supply in case of failure of a well pump in the network.
- ❑ The supply pipe network is connected to distribution network throughout the settlement.

Water Consumption

The unit of water consumption is 'Liters per capita (head) demand' or 'L.P.C.D.' for short. The product of liters per capita demand and the population of the community calculate the total demand of water for the community habitat. The demand of water is characterized by various uses of water by the community, and the cumulative demand is better known as water consumption demand. There is usually a wide variation in the total water demand among different communities. This variation depends on several factors as below:

- ❖ The conditions of the place:
  - ❑ Geographical position of the place.
  - ❑ Climatic and seasonal conditions.
  - ❑ Social and personal habits of the population.
  - ❑ The population density.
- ❖ The various uses of water by a community:
  - ❑ Domestic use: Drinking, cooking, utensils washing, house cleaning and maintenance, sewage flushing, bathing and laundering.
  - ❑ Public places and public utilities: educational institutions, public offices, transport stations, fire protection and street washing.
  - ❑ Commercial and industrial uses: stores, offices, restaurants, hotels, manufacturing establishments and electric generation.
  - ❑ For agriculture and crop irrigation.
  - ❑ During the local festivals and functions.
- ❖ Day to day basis:
  - ❑ On working days the maximum demand is in the morning between 6 to 8A.M.
  - ❑ On Sundays and holidays the maximum demand is between 8 to 10A.M.
  - ❑ In winter the demand shifts to late morning.
  - ❑ In summers the demand shifts to early morning.

An average breaks up of per capita demand as per Indian standards:

- Domestic use:
  - Drinking: 05 l.p.c.d.
  - Cooking : 10 l.p.c.d
  - Washing utensils: 15 l.p.c.d
  - House cleaning and maintenance : 10 l.p.c.d
  - Laundering: 20 l.p.c.d
  - Bathing:50;.p.c.d
  - Sewage flushing: 30 l.p.c.d

Average domestic total	**140 l.p.c.d.**
❖ Public establishments	30 l.p.c.d
❖ Industrial establishments	40 l.p.c.d
❖ Fire protection	15 l.p.c.d
❖ Losses and wastage	55 l.p.c.d
Average total	**280 l.p.c.d**

The demand factor for a place is influenced by the following factors:

- Climate.
- Class of consumers.
- Industries and commerce.
- Pressure in distribution system: more the pressure the more the more the consumption due to wastage.
- Quality of water: the better the quality the more the consumption.
- Sewage disposal system: Water borne system requires more water.
- Fires.
- Maintenance of water distribution system.

Methods of meeting variations in demands:

- Overhead tanks: are designed on average daily demand variations.
- Distribution pipes: should be designed on hourly maximum demand.
- Pumps: are designed on daily average demand.

Contaminated water: is that water, which contains suspended particles, turbidity, harmful chemicals, and bacteria, decomposed organic wastes, industrial wastes and harmful chemicals, and is not suitable for consumption.

Potable water: is the water, which can be safely used for drinking without any adverse effects and is tasty to drink.

Qualities of Potable Water

- Should be free from turbidity and sparkling transparent. Turbidity should not be more than 5ppm.
- Should be colorless, absence of metallic oxides.
- Should be odorless, absence of organic and decomposed organic matter.
- Should be cool to drink, desirable temperature should be between 5* to 13*C.
- Should be tasteful to drink. Dissolved oxygen and carbon dioxide gases make water tasteful. This explains why boiled water is tepid (tasteless).
- Should be free from harmful dissolved chemicals.
- Should be free from dissolved foul and harmful gases e.g. hydrogen sulfide, ammonia.
- Should be free from dissolved inorganic matter such as fluorides. Excess of fluorides caused softening of bones.
- Should be free from water transmitted bacteria and pathogens.
- Should be free from radioactive impurities.
- Should be free of insecticides.
- Should not be hard.
- Should contain electrolytic salts in permitted quantity.
- Ph value should be 7, i.e. should be neutral.

pH Value of water: the presence of acidic or alkali materials make the quality of water acidic or alkaline.

- Water dissociates to positive H ions and negative OH ions. The total concentration of H and OH ions is equal to 10^{-14} gm ion/liter. In neutral water H ions is equal to OH ions, therefore H ions is 10^{-7} gm ion/liter and OH ions are also 10^{-7} gm ion/liter.
- If H ions > OH ions the water will be acidic, the ph value will be 0 to 6.

If H ions < OH ions the water will be alkaline, the ph value will be 8 to14.

Hence the power of H ion concentration in solution when changed to number then is known as ph value.

Hence ph value is that negative number which, when put, as a power of 10 will indicate the H ion concentration in solution or ph = - log (H^+)

Methods of Disinfecting Water

- By boiling.

- ❖ Lime treatment.
- ❖ Bromine treatment.
- ❖ Chlorine treatment.
- ❖ Iodine treatment.
- ❖ Ozone treatment.
- ❖ Silver treatment.
- ❖ Ultra violet treatment.
- ❖ Potassium per magnate treatment.

Water treatment: Hard water and Methods of removing Water hardness

In it's raw condition water collected from the source may not be fit for human consumption due to any one or more of the following reasons:

- ❖ *Contamination*: means the presence of suspended or dissolved impurities (foreign materials) in the water. The following reasons are responsible for contamination:
  - ❑ Solid suspended impurities: fine sand, dust, clay etc.; their presence reduces the clarity of water.
  - ❑ Undesirable and harmful dissolved salts: Fluorides, chlorides, sulfates of metals, cadmium and mercury salts; their presence is responsible for coloration and organic diseases.
  - ❑ Organic materials: are present both in suspended and dissolved conditions. Sewage and decomposed matters from the dead organisms are the cause of these impurities. They impart bad odors to water.
  - ❑ Bacteria: the bacteria of water borne diseases contaminate water. The contaminated water may contain bacteria of Cholera, Dysentery, jaundice etc.
  - ❑ Industrial effluents: pesticides, acidic effluents, organic effluents, poisonous salts etc.
- ❖ Minerals: minerals are essentially inorganic salts and are needed in very minute quantities, for the body to function properly. At the same time their excess or absence in water is equally harmful and undesirable.
- ❖ Color: presence of inorganic materials or their salts are responsible for the color of water. They make water to appear bad and sometimes prove harmful and poisonous.
- ❖ Odor: presence of organic or decomposed organic materials and certain inorganic substances makes water smell bad and un-potable.

- Distasteful: absence of minerals and dissolved gases especially oxygen and carbon dioxide make water tasteless (Tepid).
- Hardness: presence of bicarbonates, chlorides and sulfates of calcium and magnesium make water hard.

Treatment of Water

It is necessary to treat the raw water to make it fit for human consumption and to improve its quality as per defined specifications and standards. A few of the main processes of the water treatment are listed below:

- Removal of suspensions: to make the water clear.
- Removal of dissolved harmful and coloring salts.
- To control the quantity of minerals.
- To destroy pathogens and bacteria present in water.
- Removal of odors and odor producing materials.
- To make water soft.

Steps in the treatment of water:

- Filtration: is the process of removing the suspended impurities. The methods depend on the size of the impurity. Some common methods are:
  - Sieving: removes big size objects both organic and debris floating in the water so that they may not get jammed up in the water pipe line and damage the pumps etc.
  - Sedimentation and decantation: the sieved water is pumped to big settling tanks. The coarse suspensions settle down and the top water slowly flows to filter tanks.
  - Gravel filter tanks: clears the next stage of coarse suspensions.
  - Sand filter: removes the turbidity or fine suspensions.
  - Coagulation and filtering: is adopted to remove micron size suspensions, which cannot be removed by the ordinary filtration processes. Some materials known as 'Coagulants' are added to water and properly mixed. The micron suspensions group together as 'Flocks', become heavier, settles down, and drained. This process makes water sparkling clear. Commonly used coagulant materials are Aluminum sulfate Al_2SO_4, $[8H_2O]$(alum), ferric chloride and ferric sulfate.

Disinfecting: disinfecting is the process carried out with the object to destroy the bacteria and pathogens. Two methods are common:

Boiling: boiling kills a wide spectrum of bacteria. The effect of the process is not long lasting. The process is time consuming and costly. It is not very practical for large-scale treatment.

Boiling removes the bicarbonate of Ca and Mg as their insoluble carbonates, and filtered. The reaction equation is as follows:

$$X(HCO3)_2 \xrightarrow{Heat} XCO_3 + H_2O + CO_2 \uparrow$$

X is Ca or Mg atom.

❖ Merits of the method:

- ❑ It is easy and neat process.
- ❑ It does not contain any chemical or chemical generated substances.
- ❑ The turbidity is easily filtered which contain the Ca and Mg carbonates.
- ❑ Carbon dioxide escapes as gas.

❖ Demerits:

- ❑ It is not a very convenient process for large quantity of water.
- ❑ It is a slow process.

Chemical treatment: the water is treated with chemicals to destroy bacteria. Caution must be exercised to the choice and the quantity of the chemical so that they do not cause harm to humans. The effect of the process is long lasting due to residual presence of the chemical in water. This process is easy to apply and cheaper. Some common chemicals:

❖ Lime, Chlorine, Bromine, Iodine and Ozone.

Lime treatment: The temporary hardness of water is measured and then treated with calculated amount of lime.

$X(HCO_3)_2 + Ca(OH)_2 \longrightarrow 2CaCO_3 + 2H_2O$ Where X = Ca or Mg atom.

The Calcium Carbonate coagulates as precipitate and filtered off.

❖ Demerits:

- ❑ It needs a large plant.
- ❑ It needs constant watch and adjustment of lime dose. The results are not up to mark.
- ❑ The flocks and wastewater requires drainage space.
- ❑ Lime is corrosive in nature.
- ❑ Lime powder makes environment dirty.

Hard water: in simple terms, hard water does not produce good 'Lather' with soap due to the presence of certain salts and as a result of this, consumes more soap.

Reasons of Hardness in Water

During precipitation, water dissolves a number of atmospheric gases, which include CO_2, Cl_2, NO_2 and SO_2. These gases being acidic inorganic oxides produce Carbonic acid, Hydrochloric acid, Nitric acid and sulfuric acid respectively in the precipitated water.

- During run off and percolation they react with the minerals present in earth and form various salts. These salts dissolve in water, out of them, the following salts are mainly responsible for water hardness:
  - Both Calcium and Magnesium Bi-Carbonates.
  - Both Chlorides and Sulfates of Calcium and Magnesium.

Types of Water Hardness

- Carbonic or Temporary hardness: Temporary hardness is due to the presence of Bi-Carbonates of Calcium and Magnesium dissolved in the water. Simple boiling of the water removes this hardness.
- Non-Carbonic or Permanent hardness: Permanent hardness is due to the present of Chloride and Sulfate of both Calcium and Magnesium. Simple boiling does not remove this hardness. Chemical or ion exchange methods are required for its removal.

Effects of Hardness on Water

- It produces less lather with soap, resulting more soap consumption.
- It produces soap scum, which produces dirty feeling during and after bath and wash.
- Causes scale formation on the inner surface of water boilers and boiling utensils. This is responsible for the corrosion of the vessel surface. It affects heat transfer rate and reduces the boiling efficiency.
- It causes turbidity during boiling of water.
- It affects the taste and structure of the cooked food.
- Too much hardness affects the digestive process.
- It affects the fabric dyeing process.

Measure and unit of hardness: The unit of hardness named 'Degree of water hardness' and is expressed as:

- 'One-degree water hardness': dissolving 14.25mgm of Calcium Bicarbonate in one kilogram of pure distilled water produces on degree hardness.
- 'One degree water hardness' is equivalent to 14.25 ppm of Calcium Bicarbonate in pure distilled water.

'One degree water hardness' is responsible for waste of 0.6 gm of Standard soap.

- Permanent hardness: permanent hardness can be removed by the following methods:

Soda ash treatment: after determining the degree of permanent hardness the water is treated with calculated amount of Sodium carbonate commonly known as soda ash. The chemical reactions are noted below:

$$XSO_4 + Na_2CO_3 \qquad XCO_3 + Na_2SO_4$$

[X = Ca or Mg atom]

$$XCl_2 + Na_2CO_3 \qquad XCO_3 + 2NaCl$$

[XCO3 precipitates]

2. Demerits: same as discussed in lime treatment.
2. **Zeolite**: Zeolite removes both permanent and temporary hardness. Zeolites are members of a family of hydrated Sodium aluminosilicate mineral [Na_2 ($Al_2Si_3O_{10}$) $2H_2O$] that contain alkali and alkaline-earth metals. Zeolites, are known for their ability toward ion exchange and reversible dehydration. The sodium ions of the zeolites are exchanged with the calcium or magnesium ions of salts responsible for water hardness:

$$Na_2\ (Z) + X\ (HCO3)2 \qquad X(Z) + 2Na\ (HCO_3)$$

$$Na_2\ (Z) + XSO_4 \qquad X\ (Z) + Na_2SO_4$$

[Z = complex part of zeolite]

$$Na_2\ (Z) + XCl2 \qquad X\ (Z) + 2NaCl$$

[X = Calcium Magnesium atom] →

This property of zeolite makes it very beneficial in softening hard water.

Zeolite Water Softeners

- These softeners are very efficient and suitable for both the temporary and permanent hardness.
- These softeners consist of 'Zeolite' or ion exchange resin in a tank connected directly to filtered hard water supply. The sodium ions of the resins change place with the calcium and magnesium ions of the Bicarbonate, chloride and sulfate salts dissolved in the water and causing temporary and permanent hardness.
- This exchange makes water soft, as the respective sodium, salts do not cause hardness.
- When calcium and magnesium ions from the water-dissolved salts, replace most of the exchangeable sodium ions of the resin; it is exhausted. Rinsing with 'Brine' (a strong solution of common salt) regenerates the exhausted resin.
- Reverse ion replacement process takes place and sodium ions from the brine now replace the calcium and magnesium ions in the exhausted resin. After washing, the regenerated resin becomes ready

for treating hard water. Repeated use of the same resin is possible.

❖ These softeners are indispensable for industries, hotels, restaurants and homes.

❖ Merit of ion exchange softener:

- ❑ They are very efficient.
- ❑ It does not produce pollution.
- ❑ The resin can be used repeatedly for long times.
- ❑ The treated water does not contain traces of treating chemicals or the resulting turbidity.
- ❑ The treated water is of good quality and potable.

Water Distribution System

There are several water–distribution system used in hospitality and catering industries:

A: Upfeed system

It is most commonly used water distribution system when the pressure of water is sufficient to force water throughout a hotel building of six floors or less in height. The maximum number of floors can be feeded with this system depends on pressure, resistance of pipe and the height of the building. (See Fig. 10.3)

B: Upfeed system with circulating pumps

This system is used when water pressure is inadequate and a circulating pump along with a return pipe (See Fig. 10.4) is installed to increase water pressure and water to flow constantly throughout the system. This is frequently used on hot–water lines to provide an adequate supply of hot water by making a provision of water heater. (See Fig. 10.5).

C: Downfeed System (Cold Water Only)

In this system first of all water is forced or pumped to a storage tank (overhead tank) located on the top floor of the building and when water is required, it flows by gravity from the storage tank to the tap. This system is used in very tall buildings. (See Fig. 10.6).

D: Downfeed Circulating System

It is very similar to the circulating puffed system. This technique is frequently used with hot water to ensure adequate amounts of hot water at each fixtures. (See Fig. 10.7).

E: Combination System

It is a combination of upfeed-downfeed system. The upfeed system is used for the lower building levels and the downfeed system for the upper

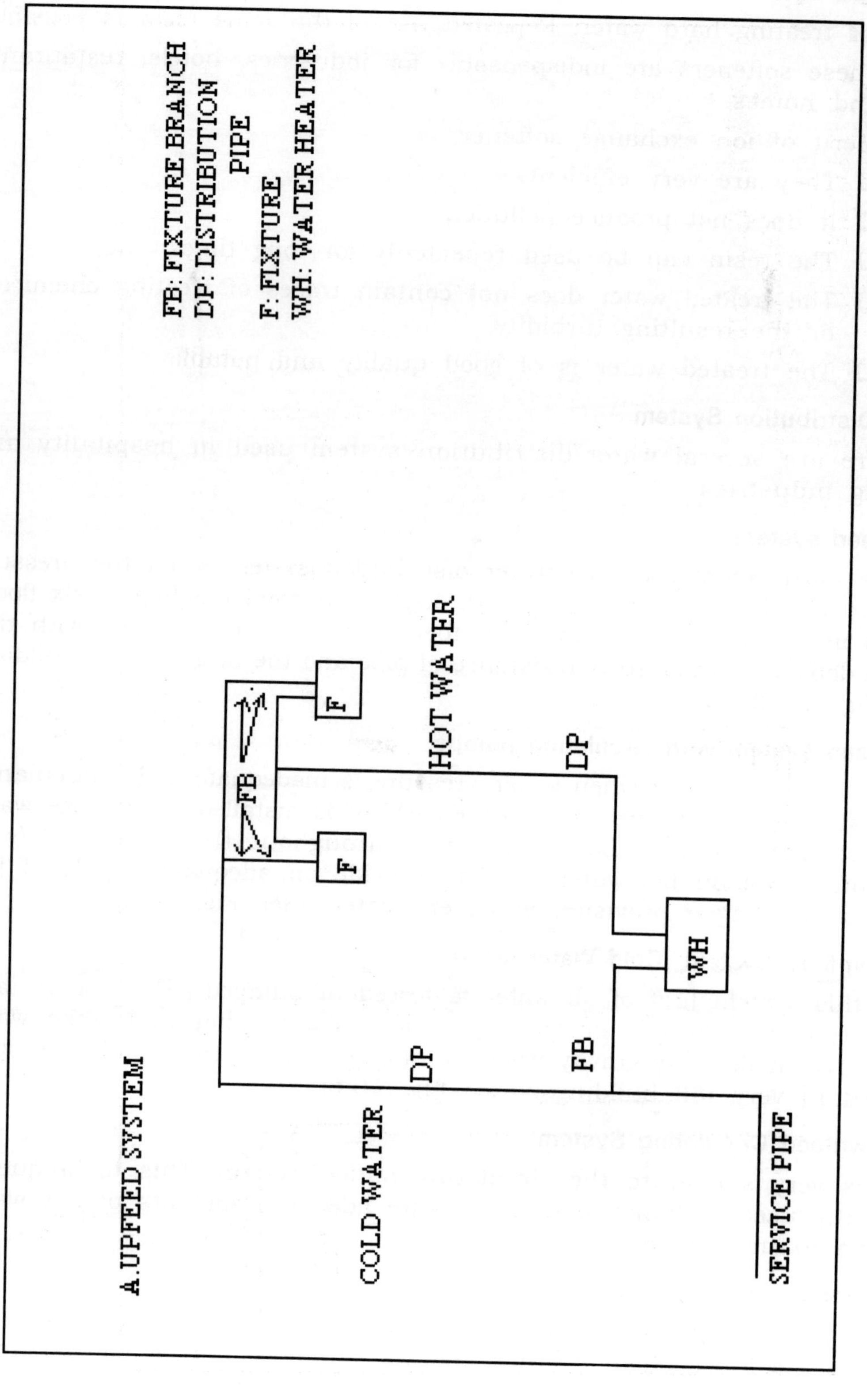
A.UPFEED SYSTEM
COLD WATER
SERVICE PIPE
DP
FB
WH
F
F
FB
DP
HOT WATER
FB: FIXTURE BRANCH
DP: DISTRIBUTION PIPE
F: FIXTURE
WH: WATER HEATER

Fig. 10.3

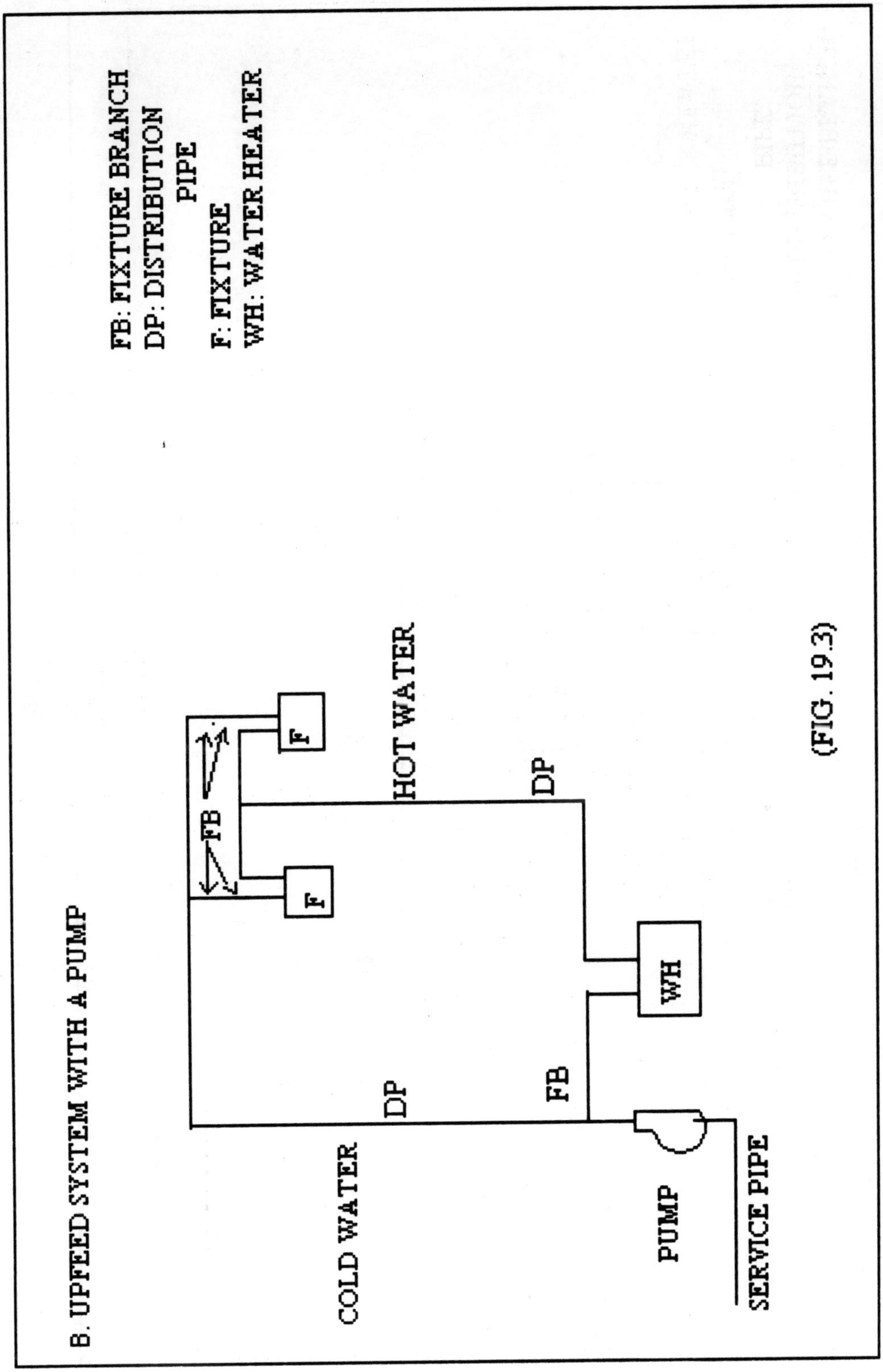
B. UPFEED SYSTEM WITH A PUMP
FB: FIXTURE BRANCH
DP: DISTRIBUTION PIPE
F: FIXTURE
WH: WATER HEATER
COLD WATER
DP
FB
PUMP
SERVICE PIPE
WH
F
F
FB
HOT WATER
DP
(FIG. 19.3)

Fig. 10.4

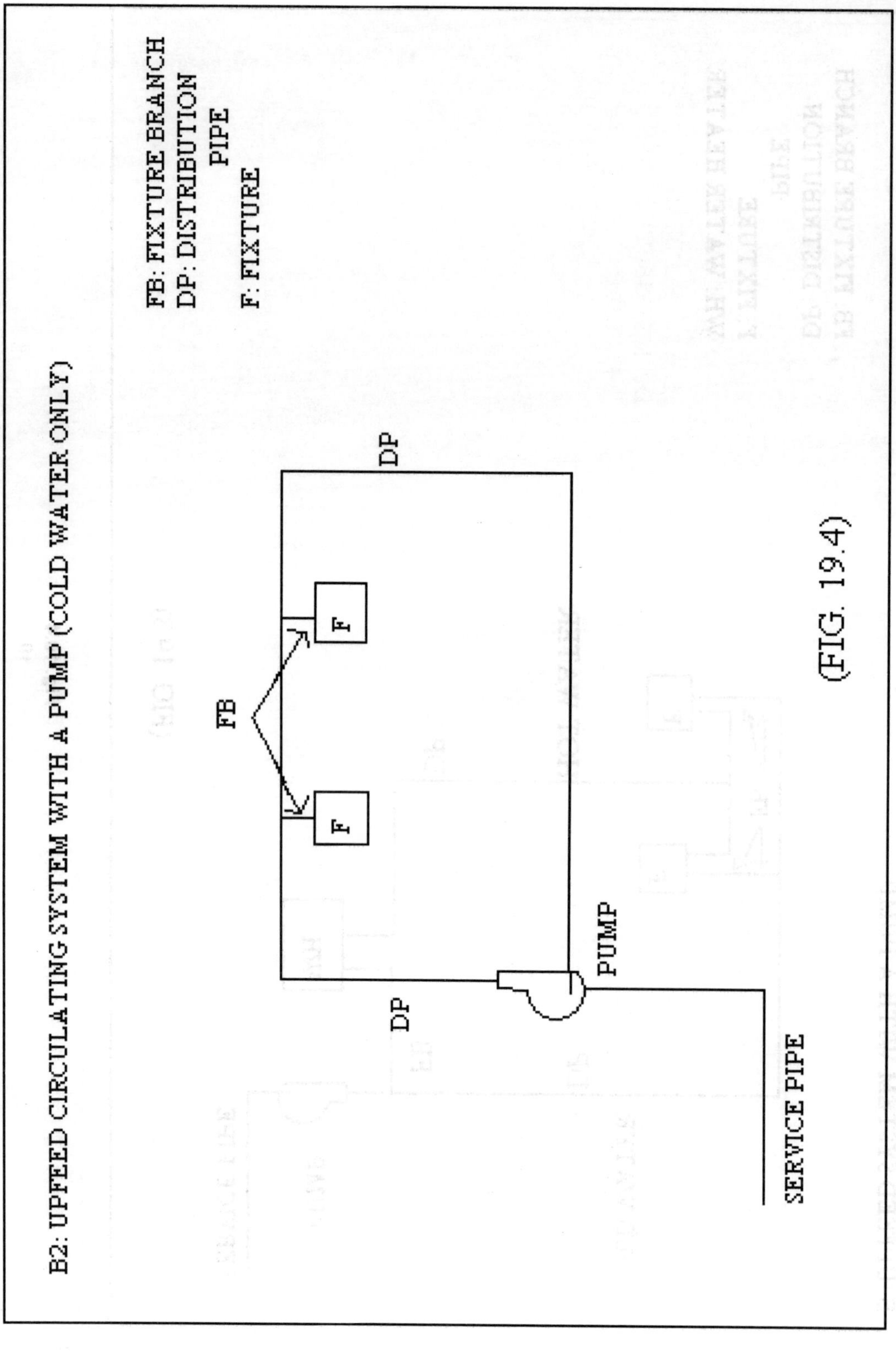
B2: UPFEED CIRCULATING SYSTEM WITH A PUMP (COLD WATER ONLY)
FB: FIXTURE BRANCH
DP: DISTRIBUTION PIPE
F: FIXTURE
DP
FB
F
F
PUMP
DP
SERVICE PIPE
(FIG. 19.4)

Fig. 10.5

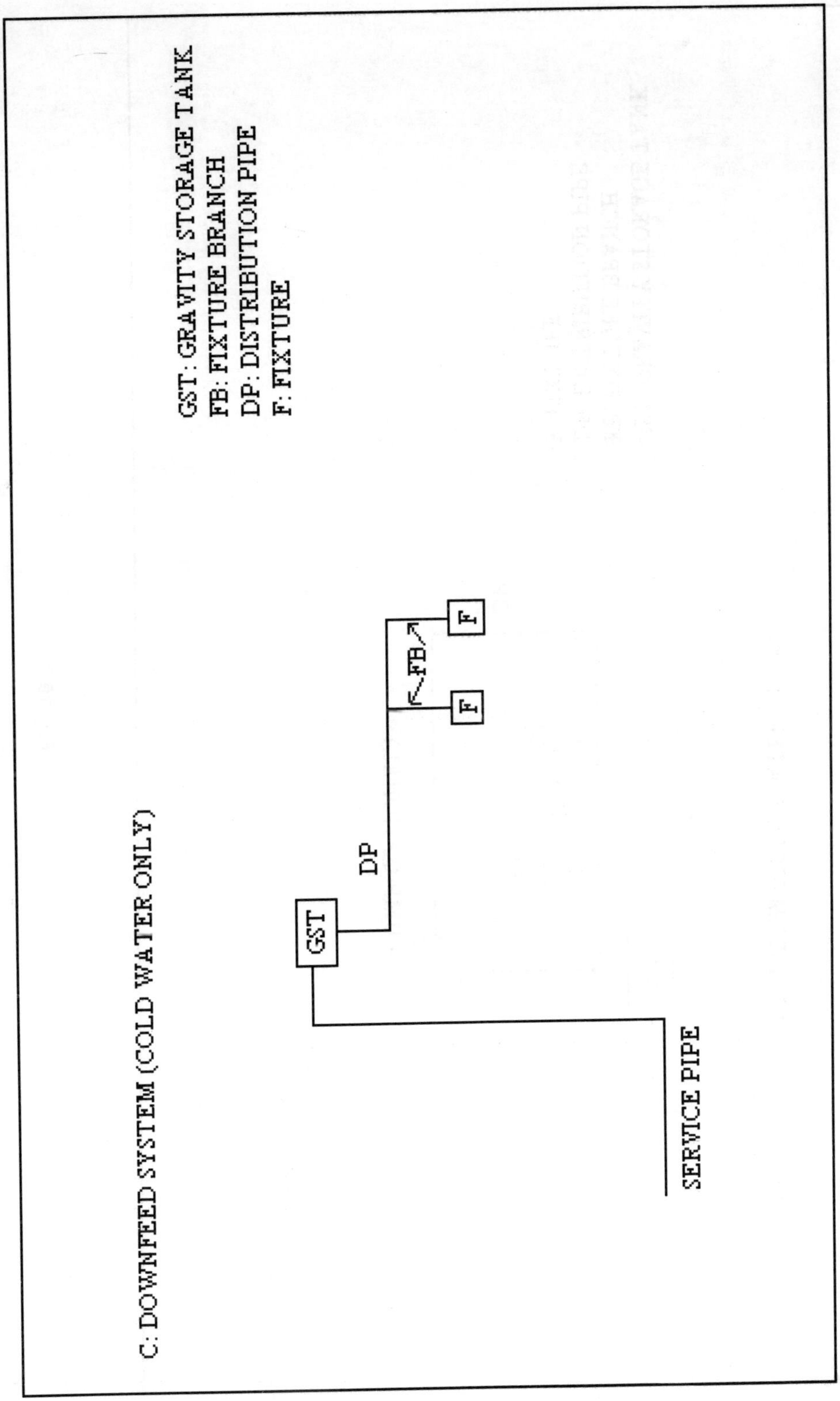
C: DOWNFEED SYSTEM (COLD WATER ONLY)
GST : GRAVITY STORAGE TANK
FB: FIXTURE BRANCH
DP: DISTRIBUTION PIPE
F: FIXTURE
GST
DP
FB
F
F
SERVICE PIPE

Fig. 10.6

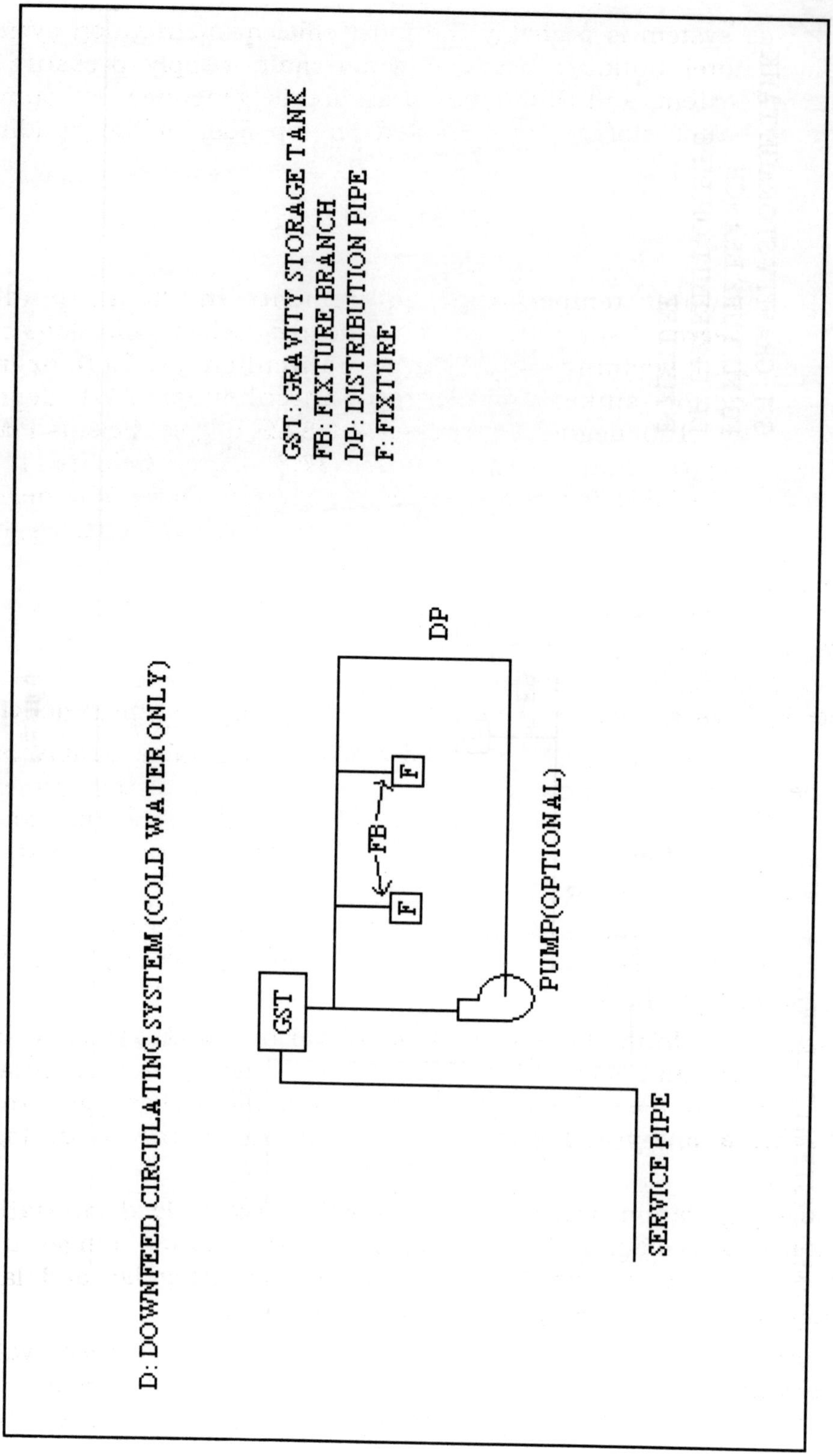
GST : GRAVITY STORAGE TANK
FB: FIXTURE BRANCH
DP: DISTRIBUTION PIPE
F: FIXTURE
D: DOWNFEED CIRCULATING SYSTEM (COLD WATER ONLY)
DP
GST
F
FB
F
PUMP(OPTIONAL)
SERVICE PIPE

Fig. 10.7

building levels. This system is probably the most efficient distribution system for multiple–floor hotel building because water–main supply pressure is utilized to the full extent and additional pressure is generated by pumps to reach water on water storage tank located on top floor of the building. (See Fig. 10.8)

Heating water

The normal hot-water temperature requirements in the hospitality industry are: 110 degree Fahrenheit or 43.3 degree Celsius for domestic use. Normal personal washing: 140 degree Fahrenheit or 60.0 degree Celsius.Food production sinks: 160 degree Fahrenheit or 71.1 degree Celsius.Dish washing: 180 degree Fahrenheit or 82.2 degree Celsius.Pools and spas: 80-100 degree Fahrenheit or 26.7- 37.8 degree Celsius. It is highly recommended to label fixtures supplied with water above 120 degree Fahrenheit or 48.9 degree Celsius with a warning that the water is hot and dangerous.

Water scarcity, under ground Water depletion and water conservation:

- Though, water may be considered an inexhaustible resource because neither any of the ecosystem processes affect the total mass of water in the ecosphere nor water is not destroyed by any biological activity.
- However, to be useful, water must be of required potable quality and should be available in sufficient quantity at the place of requirement. Due to wasteful or heavy consumption the quantity of potable water is reduced and often becomes a scarce commodity, so it must be regarded as a renewable resource.
- The useful quality and quantity of the commodity depends on the consumption and the recycle rates. The recycle time depends on the location and climatic conditions.
- Water that falls from the atmosphere as various precipitations and run off on the land surface to form streams, rivers, and eventually reaches back to feed the ocean. The repetitive process generally operates on a one-year-renewable cycle known as the 'Hydrologic cycle'.
- Unchecked population and industrial growth, large-scale deforestation are disturbing ecological conditions. This has resulted longer and disturbed water cycle time. The rains are scarce, irregular and late, causing reduction of the ground water sources.
- As the ground water sources are depleting due to disturbed water cycle. New settlements are increasing far from land water resources. Underground water sources are tapped to supply water to new

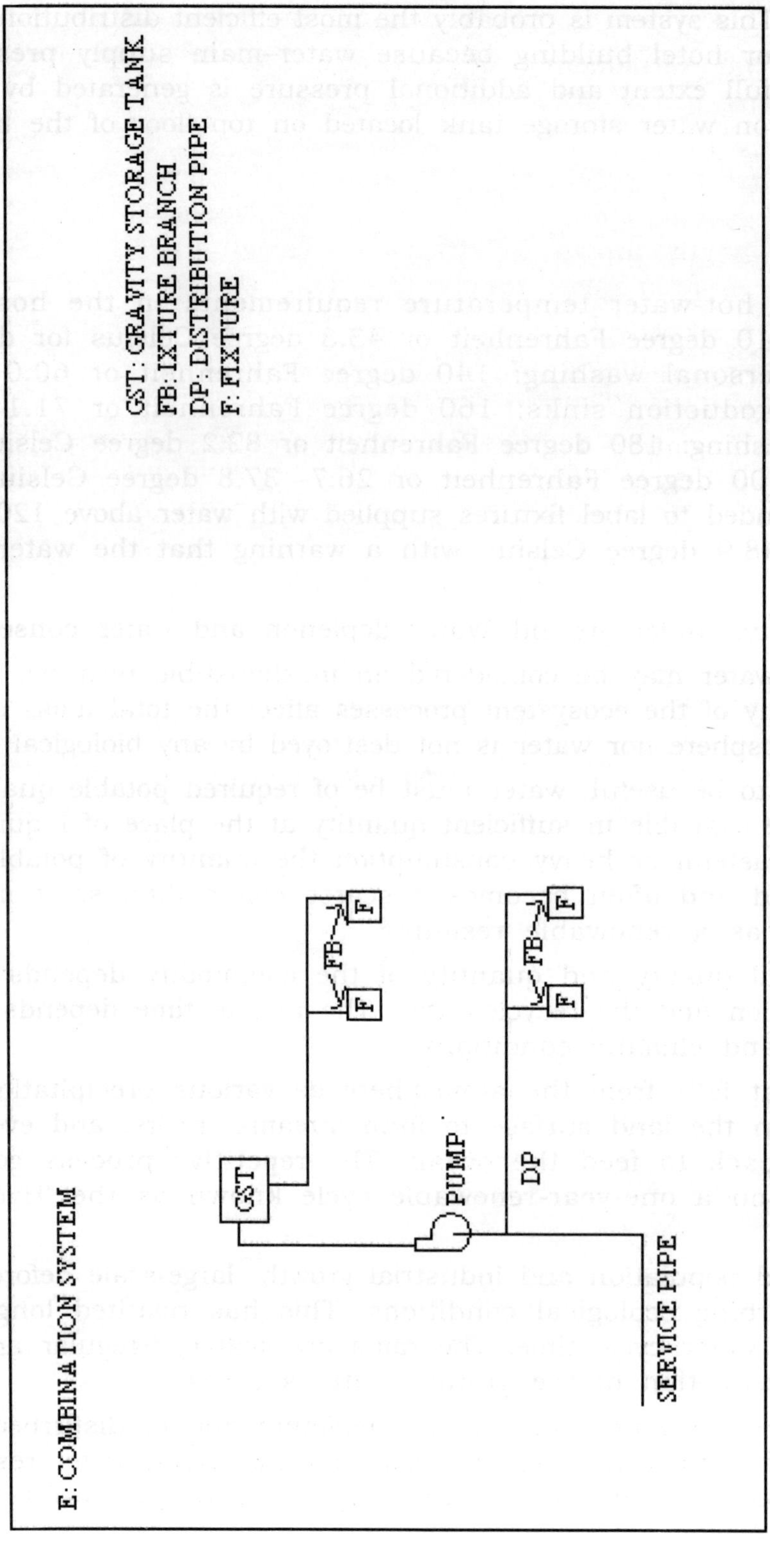
E: COMBINATION SYSTEM
GST : GRAVITY STORAGE TANK
FB: IXTURE BRANCH
DP: DISTRIBUTION PIPE
F: FIXTURE
GST
PUMP
DP
SERVICE PIPE
F
FB
F
F
FB
F

Fig. 10.8

settlements and also to supplement supplies of the growing demands of the riverside settlements. The consumption of the underground water reserves has vastly increased.

- Water percolates to underground sources very slowly. Construction of houses, roads and drains for the large populated cities has further affected the percolation area and time. The water collected at the rooftops is directly thrown in the river through the drains without getting enough area and time to percolate through the earth
- The high rate of consumption and very practically no replenishment is depleting the valuable underground water resource, which has been collected during centuries in the past.
- The present situation requires a very strict and extensive water resource management policy otherwise the vast humanity will have to suffer drinking water shortage in near future.
- When the average discharge of a river is not enough for a dependable supply of water, a conservation reservoir may be built. A dam is constructed to blocks the flow of water and allowing an artificial lake to be formed. Conservation reservoirs store water during wet-weather periods for use during times of drought and low stream flow.
- Sometimes it is advisable, for economic reasons, to provide a multipurpose reservoir. A multipurpose reservoir is designed to satisfy a combination of community needs. In addition to drinking water, the reservoir may also provide flood control, hydroelectric power, water transportation and fish farms.
- The roof top drain water of buildings in the cities should be collected in deep percolating pits or poured back into shallow wells. This helps water to percolate back to under ground reservoirs rather than waste in the drains.
- Extensive education program should be launched to educate people of the impending water shortage, and its implication on the humanity as a whole. They may be educated to reduce wastage of water on their own.
- Water conservation techniques and methods:
  - Full tap opening should be avoided.
  - Put the vessel under the tap and then open the tap.
  - Close the tap before the vessel is removed.

